LIFE S(

8 session practical guide in
Mindfulness, Meditation and Management

Robinanne Lavelle

BEc, PostGradDipEd, MEdMgt, MBusMgt *USYD*

Life Sorted: 8 session practical guide in Mindfulness, Meditation
and Management
© Robinanne Lavelle 2022

ISBN: 978-1-922644-59-6 (Paperback)
          978-1-922644-60-2 (eBook)

A catalogue record for this
book is available from the
National Library of Australia

Editors: Kristy Martin and Joanna Chalmers
Cover Design: Ocean Reeve Publishing
Design and Typeset: Ocean Reeve Publishing
Printed in Australia by Ocean Reeve Publishing and Clark & Mackay Printers

Published by Robinanne Lavelle and Ocean Reeve Publishing
www.oceanreevepublishing.com

REEVE
PUBLISHING

Disclaimer

Participants in this program should ensure that they are physically fit. Persons who suspect, or are aware of, coronary conditions or other physical fitness deficiencies should consult their doctor before undertaking this program. Individuals should proceed at their own rate. The author, publisher, producers, and distributors disclaim any liability or loss in connection with the physical and mental exercises and advice contained in this program.

Copyright Warning

Dedication

The book and audio course are dedicated to my son and his family. I hope they will utilise the knowledge gained from the study and experience to help them on their life's path, spiritual journey, and leading to a life well lived. Know that when my life is extinguished, my spirit will continue to bathe you in love from my heart.

Endorsements

The routines taught in Robinanne Lavelle's latest book 'Life Sorted', can be largely implemented into one's current daily routines. They are easy to learn and improve the quality of one's life and make it more meaningful and enjoyable. With an addition of 15-30 minutes per day practice from the audio part of the book, the listener has guided practices to calm the mind and gain wisdom and insight from within.

—Dr Charles Y Piao M.D.
PostGradDipChildHealth, MPharmacol

How do you want to live your life? This is the key question Robinanne Lavelle is asking. If you would like to live in harmony with your mind and body, then Robinanne can guide you along the road to a quality life. The eight sessions equip you with the tools to overcome the difficulties and stresses of life, to learn how to be mindful, focussed, and approach life with passion and creativity.

—Mike Campbell, BCom (Mktg) Podcaster,
Liveimmediately.com

Mindfulness is the basic human ability to be fully present, aware of where we are and what we are doing, and not overly reactive or overwhelmed by what's going on around us. The world we now live in is far from a mindful place. Robinanne Lavelle's book 'Life Sorted', is very relevant to today and teaches us that mindfulness is still available to us in every moment, from eating, to cleaning your teeth to taking a walk.

Through reading this book and practicing the techniques, you will develop self-understanding and grow in wisdom. You will learn to unleash your curiosity about yourself, both mind and heart, and develop a greater sense of warmth and kindness, both for yourself and others. You will have an improved sense of mental, physical, and spiritual wellbeing.

The eight-session course has helped me to understand my pain, lower my stress, and sleep better. This change in my life, have generated changes in other parts of my life as well. I approach tasks with greater clarity and enthusiasm having honed my ability to focus and reduced that 'tree full of drunken monkeys'. I also find myself having a sense of peace, being kinder, calmer, more patient and more playful. I am a better human being.

This text and course of activities and practices are a valuable tool for us all. The accompanying audio sessions reveal Robinanne has a beautiful voice, and the background music is a delight. The structure and organisation of the book is excellent, it is highly readable, well organised, practical, accessible, and interesting. It is a wonderful resource for people of all ages. I know my students would have benefited enormously, as would any young person. It will also appeal to those dealing with stress and distress in their lives. It has been useful to me as I have made the transition to retirement.

—Kevin Tutt, BA GradDipEd MEd Edith Cowan
Past Principal of Prince Alfred College

Acknowledgements

I would like to acknowledge the traditional custodians of country throughout Australia and their continuing connection to land, culture, and community. I pay my respects to Elders past, present, and emerging.

Audio background music by Tony O'Connor. For more information or to purchase more of Tony's music, please visit <www.tonyoconnor.com.au>.

Further Acknowledgements

I would like to thank several people for their support and guidance in my meditation practice, spiritual development, and for sharing their knowledge, which has enabled me to develop this book and audio course:

- Venerable Ajahn Jagaro, Venerable Ajahn Brahm, Abbots of Bodhinyana Buddhist Monastery, Serpentine, Western Australia
- Venerable Ajahn Vayama, Abbot of Dhammasara, Gidgegannup, Western Australia
- Father Doug Conlan, Catholic priest, Pinjarra, Western Australia
- Lidia Genovese, counselling psychologist, Perth, Western Australia
- Roger Lavell, hypnotherapist and clinical psychologist, Perth, Western Australia
- Paul Carver, clinical psychologist, Brisbane, Queensland
- Yoga teachers from the Yoga Education Society, Melbourne, Victoria
- Bambi Farrar, yoga teacher, Perth, Western Australia
- Cherrie Ray, instructor for yoga teachers, Perth, Western Australia
- Gloria Carey, Perth Naturopathic Clinic, Perth, Western Australia
- Tonia Swetman, Karratha College, for inviting me to lecture
- Philip Lavelle and Kevin Tutt for assistance with readings of the early drafts
- My friend Leoni Jenkin for initially sparking my interest in Buddhism
- My partner, son and daughter-in-law, for their constant loving support and their input during the final stage
- Ocean Reeve editors and support staff to bring this vision to reality.

Table of Contents

Desiderata

Go placidly amid the noise and the haste,
and remember what peace there may be in silence.
As far as possible, without surrender,
be on good terms with all persons.
Speak your truth quietly and clearly;
and listen to others,
even to the dull and the ignorant;
they too have their story.
Avoid loud and aggressive persons;
they are vexatious to the spirit.
If you compare yourself with others,
you may become vain or bitter,
for always there will be greater and lesser persons than yourself.
Enjoy your achievements as well as your plans.
Keep interested in your own career, however humble;
it is a real possession in the changing fortunes of time.
Exercise caution in your business affairs,
for the world is full of trickery.
But let this not blind you to what virtue there is;
many persons strive for high ideals,
and everywhere life is full of heroism.
Be yourself. Especially do not feign affection.
Neither be cynical about love,
for in the face of all aridity and disenchantment,
it is as perennial as the grass.
Take kindly the counsel of the years,

gracefully surrendering the things of youth.
Nurture strength of spirit to shield you in sudden misfortune.
But do not distress yourself with dark imaginings.
Many fears are born of fatigue and loneliness.
Beyond a wholesome discipline,
be gentle with yourself.
You are a child of the universe
no less than the trees and the stars;
you have a right to be here.
And whether or not it is clear to you,
no doubt the universe is unfolding as it should.
Therefore be at peace with God,
whatever you conceive Him to be.
And whatever your labours and aspirations,
in the noisy confusion of life,
keep peace in your soul.
With all its sham, drudgery, and broken dreams,
it is still a beautiful world.
Be cheerful. Strive to be happy.[1]

—Max Ehrmann (1872–1945)

---

1 Ehrmann, M. *Disserata A Survival Guide for Life,* 2nd edn, Andrews McMeels Publishing, Kansas City, Kansas, 2003.

Preface

Often, we are away with thoughts of the past or future and not fully experiencing the present moment. Do you have emotions come up out of nowhere? Are you stressed, unhealthy, and not happy? Having grown up with ADHD, I can particularly relate to all of these. I have come out the other side to clear thinking, focus, calmness, good health, success, joy, with a life of purpose.

Although my attention deficit has been hard, it hasn't stopped me from attending university and completing a bachelor and two masters. I've worked as a director of upper school, lectured at university, and designed a boutique child education centre. In addition, I have a passion for writing—authoring seven textbooks, a poetry book, and now this book. So how did I, the hyperactive kid who could not focus, always daydreaming in class, or getting into trouble, manage to live a successful, joyous adult life?

I left school at fourteen years of age and went to business college for a year to learn secretarial skills. Business college taught me many practical and problem-solving techniques, and the next three years of office work allowed me to put them into practice. At eighteen years of age, I returned to school to complete upper school.

Homework took me three times as long as everyone else, but I decided that my goal was far too important to give up. I learned even more about problem-solving and developed some helpful strategies to complete my education and gain acceptance into a degree in economics and politics.

As I worked through a bachelor, and then two masters (one in educational management and the other in business management), I gathered a wealth of knowledge and experience in organisation. Teaching management to upper school and university students reinforced and fine-tuned my ability to help students goal set, plan, and execute their goals, using many of the techniques I learned in management.

I was first introduced to meditation at university through yoga classes. This led me to delve more deeply into mindfulness through Buddhist meditation classes run by Theravada monks Ajahn Jagaro and Ajahn Brahm at Nollamara in Perth, Western Australia.

I attended classes every week for ten years and went on regular retreats. Additionally, I read and imbibed dozens of books on meditation, mindfulness, inspiration, spirituality, while continuing my yoga exercises and listening to dozens of Buddhist lectures that I borrowed from the Nollamara Buddhist library. I travelled to Thailand and went to the Buddhist jungle monastery Ubon Ratachani, where the monks who taught me had trained.

I have since worked with many people to reach their potential. When teaching high school, I worked with students diagnosed with ADHD. I found ways to help them when colleagues could not. I understood where they were coming from. During this time, I also ran after-hours TAFE classes for adults wanting to be more organised, mindful, and focused as they were struggling, often in situations where they were self-employed running small businesses.

I have been using mindfulness and meditation for many decades and know the benefits of practising daily. By my mid-thirties, I was running mindfulness and meditation courses at a tertiary college, working with students from sixteen to sixty years of age. Some of my students had phobias; others were stressed, had depression, or were overwhelmed with their responsibilities. While teaching these students, I was inspired to write Meditation: Creating Quality Life.[2] This was a book and accompanying audio sessions, designed to assist the student studying this course.

I found it helpful to tailor my students' practice to meet individual needs. For example, a person with ADHD may only handle five minutes of any of the practices for quite some time, as they must deal with an exceptionally busy mind and a body that wants to keep active.

I have created this short course to help build your organisational skills and execute a more enjoyable, calm, positive, successful life. You don't need to have ADHD to benefit from this course; it can help anyone learn how to become mindful, organised, and focused.

---

2 Lavelle, R., *Mediation: Creating Quality Life*, 1st edn, Tranquil Retreat Creations, Perth, 1994.

Introduction

This book is a self-training practical course that teaches mindfulness exercises and meditation practices to improve your life experience. Over the years, I have found that students come to this course for many different reasons. Some come for relaxation, others for relief from their stressful lives or partnerships, some have phobias or disorders, while many are drawn to the peacefulness or seek a higher level of being and spirituality.

People often commence my course by asking, 'How can mindfulness, meditation, and management benefit me?' My students have reported several benefits after completing this course material:

- improved concentration
- reduced stress
- sounder sleep
- heightened awareness.

If you would like to address any or all these aspects of your life, then this course is for you. Learning these mindfulness exercises, meditation practices, and management techniques will improve your life experience. This course aims to improve four different areas of your life:

1. managing your life
2. health and wellbeing
3. relationships with others
4. your essence.

The course has eight sessions, and each session has several mindfulness exercises, audio-guided meditation practice, and management strategies. The eight sessions are:

1. Introduction to Mindfulness and Meditation
2. Overcoming Difficulties
3. Active Meditation
4. Reducing Stress
5. Creative Visualisation
6. Wellbeing
7. The Soul and the Spirit
8. Summary.

Each session in the book has three parts:

1. Explanation
2. Mindfulness and Management Exercises
3. Meditation Practice.

Whatever its initial state, the mind can be tamed through dedication, determination, and a willingness to be happy with incremental achievement. Be kind to yourself and do not measure yourself against others' progress, as you may have a lot more to overcome. There are riches to be had by all at everyone's own pace. Be patient and resolute to keep persevering.

Max Ehrmann aptly sums this up in his poem *Desiderata* (things to be desired):

> *'If you compare yourself with others, you may become vain or bitter, for always there will be greater and lesser persons than yourself. Enjoy your achievements ...'*[3]

The entire poem *Desiderata* put to music by Les Crane is a wonderful rendition and a great way to start any day!

---

3 Ehrmann, M. *Disserata A Survival Guide for Life,* 2nd edn, Andrews McMeels Publishing, Kansas City, Kansas, 2003.

Session 1: Introduction to Mindfulness and Meditation

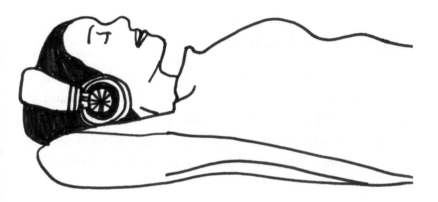

Analogy for Your Life

A monk once told me a story about the dung beetle. Dung beetles play a critical role in Australia's grazing ecosystem as they roll revolting piles of cow poo into small balls that they then bury in the soil. They spend their lives up to their eyeballs in poo, working with the manure all day long, rolling it, pushing it, and ultimately trying to get rid of it! Do you sometimes feel you spend your days pushing excrement uphill? If you are the dung beetle, you have no appreciation of the world outside of poo! Dung beetles are not aware of the wonders surrounding them away from the dung.

This can be an analogy for one's life. If you are living your life in an unfocused, disorganised, unaware way, then it could feel like you are in the poo all the time. Possibly you, or your parents, or your partner, or friends have a glimpse of what your life could be like if only you got it sorted.

This course is designed to still the busy mind and help you learn techniques that get your life together. Over eight weeks, you will complete one session each week and use the rest of the week to revise what you have learned through the readings, stories, mindful exercises, and repeating the meditation practices.

Origins of the Practices

Throughout this course, we will use mindful mental exercises that you can use in your daily routines to prepare for deeper states of meditation, leading to a calm, alert, focused, and insightful mind. Mindfulness and meditation practices have been used for thousands of years and here follows a short background of the practices for your appreciation.

Yoga Meditation

Yoga was developed in northern India some 5,000 years ago but could be up to 10,000 years old. Some of these techniques are used in the meditation practices in the audio sessions accompanying this book. Meditation in yoga is usually performed in the prone position or the basic sitting position. 'Yoga is like music. The rhythm of the body, the melody of the mind, and the harmony of the soul create the symphony of life' (BKS Iyengar).[4] The teaching was designed to sacrifice ego through knowledge of the inner self and understand that there is karma (actions lead to reactions, that is, cause and consequence) with the aim that one should always be moving towards greater wisdom.

---

4 B.K.S. Iyengar, *The Meaning of Life—The Harmony of Body, Mind and Soul*. Excellence Reporter, France, Beziers, February 10, 2020 https:// excellencereporter.com

Buddhist Meditation

Buddhism is not a religion but a philosophy. There is no mention of God in the studies, but that does not mean you cannot study religion while practising meditation. Thus, a Catholic priest could, in principle, undertake Buddhist meditation.

Buddhism was founded in India in the sixth century BC by Prince Siddhartha. He was brought up in a palace shielded from the suffering of people outside the walls. On venturing outside, he was shocked at what he saw, so he set off on a lone crusade to examine the meaning of life.

After many years of trying different paths and practices, Prince Siddhartha (the Buddha) found a pathway to enlightenment through what he called a middle path not involving the extreme practices of the ascetics. He tried to help other people achieve this enlightened state.

During his lifetime, he discovered the noble truths: the truth of suffering, the truth of the cause of suffering, the truth of the end of suffering, and the truth of the path that leads to the end of suffering. He became aware of the need to understand that everything is impermanent and changing and that understanding this would end suffering.

To help people end their suffering, he developed a pathway for people to follow. The path incorporates the following:

1. correct view
2. correct intention
3. correct speech
4. correct action
5. correct livelihood
6. correct effort
7. correct mindfulness
8. correct concentration.

These elements of the eightfold path are qualities to be developed in the mind of a person seeking to achieve the highest state of wisdom, happiness, and ultimately enlightenment.

Transcendental Meditation

Another form of meditation is Transcendental Meditation (TM). Although the monk Maharishi understood the broadness of Hinduism, he was charged to use just the practice of TM across the world in an endeavour to create world peace. The practice is for anyone as it is not a religious ritual but a mental practice.

TM first spread from India to the West in the mid-1900s and was then made popular by the pop band, The Beatles, who were followers of this type of meditation. Each member of the Beatles was given an individual mantra—a sound the meditator repeats, which assists in blocking unwanted thoughts from coming into the mind at random, helps to calm the mind, and achieves a higher sense of focus. You will not be given an individual mantra in this course; however, repetition of certain words will be used at times to help focus the mind.

Social Change

Meditative paths tend to focus on developing the inner self instead of outward signs of wealth and status. Our materialist society with little attachment to nature has possibly enhanced our dissatisfaction with life. Material possessions often give us little joy as people seek bigger and better than what they already have. How many updates have you made to your television, furniture, car? Were they at a point where they needed replacement because they were old and broken, or were you just updating to be fashionable? We measure our success by having the latest of everything and do not judge success by our quality of mind or the good deeds we do.

Coupled with this is the problem that we are connected twenty-four seven. Our electronic devices can mean we are never off the grid. Workers can be contacted at home on their mobile, and social media has created an addiction, so we want to be updated all the time. We seem to be living life in a faster lane now, and it appears to be getting faster. No downtime leads to stress!

We work hard, party hard, and have great toys. Many employees take work home or stay late at work to meet expectations. Working so hard sometimes means people have the same attitude to leisure time. They work out at top speed at the gym, they drink and eat to excess at a restaurant. Their relationships are transitory as they superficially connect to others. They have no time! Even our garden is not a restful place as we are more likely to be working in it than just enjoying and soaking up being present with nature. We are building pergolas, putting in pools, landscaping the garden, and mowing lawn that is rarely used as we rush around, creating a better (but not happier) life.

In early 2020, we were forced to stop, and being confined for long periods to one's house allowed us to pause and reflect on what is important to us, what we value, who we want to be, what we want to do with our life. It has been a time of many seeking new career paths as they had time to evaluate their work life and whether it was fulfilling. Thus, a positive outcome from the terrible Coronavirus was that individuals started to seek a more meaningful existence. Mindfulness and meditation are pathways to this self-investigation that is richer than material possessions. So, meditation classes have increased in number as a result during this period.

Relaxation and Meditation

People often think that the words relaxation and meditation are synonymous. They think that if you are doing a relaxation technique, then you are meditating. However, this is not the case. For example, one form of relaxation could be lying on your living room floor listening to your favourite music. While lying there, enjoying the music, you allow your mind to wander as your body relaxes. This is rejuvenating, but this is not meditation.

In a meditative state, we are alert, awake, and mindful. It is the complete opposite of relaxation, sleep, or daydreaming. Relaxation is a helpful technique to use when learning to take the mind and body to a state of meditation. Relaxation is only the preparation or the starting point to a meditative practice. Guided practice can take you on a mental journey through a forest or to the sea, and visualising one scene helps prevent random, unhelpful, busy thoughts disturbing one's focus.

Meditation, at its ultimate, is where our practice moves beyond the meditation object, where we are focused, alert, awake, and observing our thoughts from a point where we have let go and are detached. It is a place of bliss, amazement, and profound wisdom where the mind is trained and disciplined, acting at its highest level. Having developed the ability to achieve this point through practice, the mind has a higher level of focus and peacefulness throughout one's daily life and not just during a formal meditation session.

Such practices require a willingness to take pleasure in focusing. For this reason, it is a good idea not to meditate in a place you normally relate to sleep. Make sure you do not feel overly tired. You will become despondent if you fall asleep during the meditation as little will be achieved. Choose a time when you are ready to put in the effort to achieve wonderful results.

In the audio-guided practice, the first objective is to teach you to relax, as this is good preparation for the meditation. Learning relaxation techniques is a process necessary to take you to the heart of the matter, that is, to focus the mind to concentrate on one thing at a time; to train the mind not to deviate or allow random thoughts to disturb you. At this achieved state, you will be absorbed inwardly, with a mind that is fully aroused and aware.

As a result of meditating, you will start to see that you are carrying out everything in a far superior manner. At work, a problem will be solved more efficiently and with less stress. In your personal life, you will listen more clearly to your loved ones and enjoy what you are doing in a more meaningful way. The emphasis in the course will be to train the mind on what you are doing at that precise moment in time, and as a result, develop calmness and clarity in your daily life.

Stressful Mind

To meditate successfully, we cannot just focus on the mind; we must also look at the body. You are probably aware that stress eventually manifests itself in physical illness or disease. The origin of the word disease is *desaise,* which means lack of ease derived from Old French:

des (expressing reversal) + *aise* (ease) = *desaise* (lack of ease).

Thus, the close relationship between mind and body cannot be ignored. Hence, yoga and meditation are now being recommended by doctors for many illnesses such as heart conditions.

The mind is present when we are alive; it is our ability to think and perceive. We are normally only aware of the conscious level of our mind and mostly unaware of the subconscious. Considerable distress and tension can manifest in the subconscious mind, the mind that may not be present is restless, obsessed, and anxious.

Now would be a good time to look at your mind. What state is it in? Is your mind peaceful? Are you fixed on what you are doing at this precise moment? Cast your mind back. How many other random thoughts have you allowed to disrupt your concentration, like, *I shouldn't be reading this right now; I need to do some chores.*

What thoughts do we have in a day? We spend an incredible amount of time planning this and that and worrying over what we did or did not do. Many people's psyches have become hyperactive, always living in the past or future but not the present. The brain on hyperdrive can't drill down into one problem as it jumps all over the place.

Developing insight and wisdom from such an undisciplined mind is problematic. No wonder at the end of the day, we feel exhausted and reach for the bottle or screen as a form of escapism. Thus, not physically exhausted at the end of the day but mentally exhausted from the continual, erratic flow of thoughts we allow to come in. This state of constant chatter is like a tree of drunken monkeys. Meditation will help train this 'monkey mind' to be disciplined and of great assistance to you. Otherwise, the untrained mind does a lot of damage, much more harm than anyone else can do to you.

What state is your mind in now? Do you have a raging storm within, or a clear, peaceful pond in which to bathe your thoughts? If you train your intellect, it will be like a clear pond, still and peaceful, where you will be able to see all the way to the bottom, and from this place of clarity, good thoughts, actions, and intentions arise. If you have a continual storm brewing, you will not be able to make decisions, as you cannot see solutions in the dark, wind-swept storm, where you are blown here, there, and everywhere.

Exercise 1—Peaceful Mind

Close your eyes and imagine you are in a peaceful place—floating safely and easily in a crystal-clear lake.

1. Observe the still water; there is no breeze to disturb the stillness.
2. Look into the clear water; you can see right to the bottom of the pool.
3. Sit with that image for a moment.

4. Now, imagine the water is full of rubbish and pollutants; you can't see what's below the surface.
5. Picture a howling gale; the water becomes murkier and turbulent. You are being pushed in a direction that you didn't choose.
6. Open your eyes.

Reflect on which pool you want your mind to dwell—the calm, clear, peaceful water with no pollutants or the murky, stormy water? A clear mind will invite clarity; a murky mind will create a cluttered array of thoughts.

Most of us spend much of our time daydreaming, with thoughts often coming in haphazardly. When we are caught up in the judgements, points of view, and feelings about the past and future, we forget how to experience the here and now. Therefore, we rarely experience the reality of life. The saying, 'The lights are on, but no one is home' is an apt description of how many people live much of their busy lives. The idea of meditation is to discipline the mind not to meander but to maintain our attention on one thing. The mind will try to run off at any moment; we must watch it, be aware of what is happening, and bring the mind back to the clear pond.

We can understand this undisciplined mind if we relate it to a boat on the ocean. If we have lost sight of land and are unable to anchor, we cannot see if our boat is drifting this way or that. However, if we suddenly catch sight of land, we can get our bearings and realise that we are coasting one way or the other and do something about it.

In the following meditation exercise, we will use the breath like the land, an anchor to notice if we are moving one way or the other. Concentrating on the breath will ensure that we notice the moment that ideas, thoughts, and judgements start creeping in; be able to notice this, and return to the breath and focus, even if only for a second or two.

If you are in a place where your mind never feels anchored, and you feel all at sea, then your current situation may be the cause. It might be the result of you ending a relationship, losing your job, or any other cause of grief. When my mother died, I felt lost, like I no longer had an anchor. My way forward had vanished, and my mind was all over the place. I had already lost my father a few years earlier. I felt sad when Dad died but devastated when Mum died. I told a friend that I could not understand why I felt so lost now, especially as I was more attached to my father but had taken his passing far better. My friend, who had already lost his parents, was spot on when he said that it wasn't just about losing my mother, it was now about losing my parents, as a whole generation had now passed.

I've now learned that when you feel like this (lost and all at sea!), don't do anything or change your life in any way; sit with it and be with it. The mistake I made was to listen to my boyfriend at the time and agree to move in with him. I was vulnerable, emotional, and ended up with what turned out to be a dangerous partner. I now use the mantra 'do nothing when I'm not sure what to do'. Wait until clarity and wisdom arise to give a clear direction.

I needed to go through the seven stages of grieving: shock, denial, anger, bargaining, sadness, reconstruction, and acceptance in my own space and time. If you want to learn more about how a person grieves and how to move through and out the other side with insight, integration, and grace, you might like to read Megan Devine's book, *It's Ok That You're Not Ok*.

Instead of adjusting to the loss of my parents through these stages, I made the mistake of moving in with my boyfriend when I was still at the shock stage. So, then I had to live with the emotional fallout from a coercive, controlling, gaslighting, and abusive partner, as well as try to work through the grief of losing my parents.

On reflection, I should have stayed where I was and allowed for healing; then I would have been ready for a healthy relationship. Devine's book title also alludes to the idea that one should get their life sorted before contemplating entering a new relationship or moving to a more committed stage within a relationship. It would have saved me the emotionally scarring and post-traumatic stress that I suffered.

What we want to build is a calm and still mind and a connected, worthwhile, happy, and emotionally-mature person. So, try not to become disillusioned if your mind feels all at sea when your mind jumps all over the place. Remember that your psyche has had years of experience wandering, so the very old saying, 'Rome wasn't built in a day' is a good attitude to have when you are having difficulties with the practice. The fact that you are aware that the mind has drifted off is a good thing; it's the start of the journey. To become aware is halfway to dealing with the situation.

Exercise 2—Moments of Peace

Start this exercise by centring all your attention on your breath. If you can only concentrate and be peaceful for the count of one or two seconds, it becomes clear that prior to learning to meditate, you had a busy, inefficient mind, which wandered aimlessly. Just watch your breath going in, watch your breath going out. Become at one with the breath as if nothing else matters during this exercise. Some people can hold on to this anchor, the breath, for longer than one or two breaths.

Where you start is unimportant, and progress at your own rate. Do not become vain or bitter by comparing your progress to others, as this will be your ego speaking. Just put your ego aside and direct your attention to the breath without judgement. Try to extend the length of time that you are mindful, peaceful, focused on the breath, and concentrating on one thing.

The moment you notice a thought, merely be aware of it; try not to allow yourself to continue the thought pattern. For example, if you catch yourself thinking, *Oh that's right, I have to do such and such today*, bring yourself back to the breath by saying, *No, I don't want to think about that at present, I am concentrating on the breath.* If another thought comes in, calmly and with gentle effort, bring yourself back to your breathing. Remember, your breath is your anchor allowing you to observe thoughts coming into the mind and giving you the space to not contemplate these thoughts but send them on their way. If it helps, visualise yourself using your hand to gently wipe the thought from your mind.

Concentrate on the Breath

Much of the distinction in meditation forms are brought about by the different objects of focus initially used in meditation. However, the aims are similar, to centre the mind so you are the observer of the mind, not merely a victim of thoughts running all over the place.

Some techniques (yoga) use the breath as the meditation object. The breath becomes the focus of your attention, watching the natural flow of breathing. One needs to relax, not regulate the breath in any way, just observe as a breath arises and then falls. If your breath becomes shallow and then alters to become quite deep, allow this to happen. If the breath is maintained as rhythmic, then allow this to happen too. Do not place any value judgement on how you should be breathing during this practice. It is important that we are here only as non-judgemental observers.

Lying down and focusing on the breath may not be easy. It takes effort to train the undisciplined mind. This should not be a forced effort but takes patience and continued gentle perseverance. In this early session of lying in the prone position on the floor (or thin mat), the effort will be on relaxing every muscle in your body and bringing your body to a state of ease. Only after the muscles are fully relaxed do we move on to meditation on the breath. We become more peaceful once fixing onto the breath.

Place and Equipment for Relaxation

It is important to choose a place where you are going to undertake the practical sessions. Ensure you have safe surroundings. Choose a place in your home where you will not be disturbed. This may involve discussing with those in the house a time and space where you will not have to hear other noises. For example, if you have a baby or small child, you might choose a time when you know they are sleeping or arrange for another adult to take the child for a walk during this special time.

A thin roll-out piece of foam is a great base to use for the prone position relaxation technique. You could also fold a quilt on the floor. It is important not to use a pillow of any sort. The pillow will raise your head, and for a successful relaxation session, it is important to have the spine in line and flat on the floor. You may like to have a blanket over you as the body tends to drop in temperature due to the stillness of this practice. If you are concerned that using a blanket will trigger sleep, then an alternative is to have a heater on in the room.

In the early stages of this practice, it is important not to be distracted. Later, when you have learned to focus, you will be able to block out sounds that could distract you, for example, the voices of people in the background, cars passing by, etc. Think about what might distract you before you start and try to ensure they will not interrupt you. For example, turn off your mobile phone and/or put a note on the door to your room so no one disturbs you.

As you progress in the practice, you will notice that you are unaware of outside influences and able to focus on the breath, even amidst chaos. As you become more skilled, it could be helpful to add a degree of outside noise and see if you can rise above it. For example, the next-door neighbour's dogs always bark in the afternoon, so you could time your practice then. You could use this to develop your skill. Remember, you choose for the noise of barking to annoy you. Your mind goes to the noise and brings it back to within you. Detach yourself from the noise of the barking dog and go inward.

A monk told a story about a young novice who was frustrated with learning to meditate, so the senior monk sent him to the markets to practice. He had to sit amidst all the noise and try to focus on the breath. This was indeed a tough gig! We won't do such a hard-core approach, but build up gradually towards the ability to detach from external disturbances.

Another monk told me that a young monk was told to sit near an ant mound to meditate. He had ants crawling all over him and biting him as he fought to maintain his focus on the breath. Eventually, the young monk came to realise he had to let go, to be at one with the ants. This was when the ants stopped biting him and used his body as if it were the ground; to traverse to get to where they were going. There was no resistance, no nervous energy emitting from the monk. It is in this state of surrender, giving in, falling back from pushing that the monk found connection and peace with all that surrounded him.

If outside noises are too difficult to ignore, you might like to have gentle music playing in the background. These might merely be sounds of nature, such as a waterfall, whales singing, a babbling brook, or peaceful instrumental background music. When listening to natural sounds or soft music, you can allow the sound to wash over you to trigger relaxation and assist you to let the constant thought patterns dissipate. I don't suggest you sit in meditation at a marketplace or near an ant's nest, at this stage!

Audio Practical Session 1: Basic Prone Position Relaxation—Focus on the Breath

You are now ready to listen to the practical session available on the audio recording. Repeat this session many times over the week at a set time.

Session 2: Overcoming Difficulties

Insufficient Time

I knew I had trouble with time. I recall when my girlfriend and her husband and two children knocked on our door at 6 pm one summer Saturday evening. Surprised they were there but trying to be polite, I said, 'Oh, nice of you to drop by.'

'You invited us to dinner a fortnight ago,' my friend answered.

Being caught up with other things, I had totally forgotten and did not even have any dinner cooking. I felt so embarrassed. I knew something had to change.

Placing a thirty-day monthly calendar whiteboard in the kitchen was the start to organising my personal life. When I put on the jug for my hot chocolate last thing at night and then again for my morning coffee, I always look up at the board and see what I have got on that day and later in the week. Nowadays, I can be doubly aware of appointments/arrangements because I also pop them into my mobile phone calendar and set an alarm for one hour prior to remind me. All this helps time management of my personal life.

In my work life, I use a business diary open on my work desk. The diary has the week in view over the open two-page spread. At the end of the day, I pop any appointments into my mobile phone from the diary. When talking on the phone or to staff, I immediately write anything I need to do into the diary. Time can be managed! Being late all the time is stressful, and it is far better to put a system in place that alleviates the worry about time. Can you allocate a time to work on these exercises and practices and pop appointments onto your whiteboard calendar, mobile phone, or diary (or all three)?

The main problem I have heard from students is, 'How can I find the time to include meditation in my busy life?' They say their life is too busy to spare thirty to forty minutes per day developing the art of meditation. One activity I ask my students to engage in when evaluating whether they have enough time is to ask them what they would do if they were told they only had one hour to live. I doubt very much that they would vacuum the floor or pay the bills or do the shopping! Most people would spend the last hour of their lives doing what is enjoyable or meaningful to them. Yet, we sometimes spend hours, weeks, or even months doing things that are not meaningful to us! We are often caught up in the rut of habitual conditioning.

I am not suggesting that we suddenly abandon all our responsibilities in life, but consider what is essential for our souls and wellbeing. In fact, the moment you hear yourself saying, 'I should', consider changing it to 'I could', and then contemplate and decide whether you will do it. 'Should' implies a value judgement imposed on us from outside influences. For example, I could vacuum the floor, but I am doing it more out of habit than necessity, or use it for procrastination. Busy work may stop you from making the time to look after yourself with these exercises and practices.

A useful tool to find time is time management, which requires learning to employ time more efficiently. Some people have an aversion to time management without understanding the concept. They think they would rather act spontaneously and carry out tasks as the need arises. I often ask how these people feel when numerous jobs have accumulated, and all need doing urgently. A feeling of coping comes from keeping on top of the mundane by using a strategic plan. From this organised state comes the opportunity for spontaneous activities, without the guilt!

Here is a simple example of time management that I have found works. I could clean the toilet today and the bathroom tomorrow, but it will take less time if I clean both and include the laundry too. They all use the same cleaning products and equipment, which I only need to get out once to do it all at the same time.

I also found it more efficient if my partner did the shopping and brought home takeaway dinner while I cleaned the house, instead of us both going to the shops and then both trying to clean. He was more efficient at shopping and loved the social interactions, whereas I loved the quiet of cleaning the house.

Even our child was involved. He was taught how to strip his bed, put on clean sheets, take down his towel, and put it all in the washing machine, and when it was finished, hang it out on the line (with help from Mum). He could then set the table ready for dinner when his dad got home with the special Friday night takeaway. This taught our son routines and expectations of how to manage time and be responsible. Additionally, many hands make light work.

Household Time Management

Time management requires planning for it to be successful. This can be achieved by everyone in your household helping to set the plan by following these easy steps:

1. Brainstorm
2. Allocate time
3. Distribute tasks
4. Start a reward system.

Brainstorm

Sit down as a family and brainstorm the duties that must be covered in the home. Your list might look something like the following:

- **Clothes:** washing, hanging out, sorting, ironing, and folding away
- **Kitchen**: preparation, cooking, dishwasher, cleaning kitchen, dish washing
- **House**: tidying, dusting, vacuuming and mopping, cleaning wet areas
- **Outside**: watering and pruning garden, washing the car, mowing the lawn, cleaning the windows, doggie poos
- **Shopping**: shopping list, food, chemist, etc., and packing it away at home
- **Bills**: banking, paying bills, keeping track of the budget, setting up auto deductions.

Allocate Time

Together allocate a length of time you think each duty takes each week, for example, cooking 4.5 hours per week and window washing 0.5 hours per week (because you would only do one window weekly or maybe do the house monthly running up two hours). It may work more effectively if everyone works at the same time. For example, two children might be responsible for changing all the linen while one adult cleans the house and the other does the weekly shopping.

Distribute Tasks

Ask each member of the household what job/s they would like and distribute the workload equitably. Have each person commit to a time and day of the week they will perform their responsibility and enter this onto the weekly planner that could then go on the fridge.

Every month, you could change over who does what so you are teaching your children important life skills across a range of areas.

Start a Reward System

Building in a reward at the end of the chores might work well too. For example, after the chores, make it a special weekly night with takeaway dinner, a drink with friends, or a family board game.

Workplace Time Management

Although I have used the example of home life to show how time management can work, it can also be used in the workplace to ensure you are more productive onsite, taking less work home, thus freeing up some time for meditation and caring for your wellbeing. Of course, a crisis can happen, but with a regular plan of attack, it is more likely that you will keep on top of your work. A well-organised person will endeavour to have some sort of plan for their working life, so each day is utilised effectively.

It is also important to know and respond to your body clock and biorhythms. For example, if you are a night owl who likes to start work late and finish late, maybe you could find a job that suits your hours. I have a friend who works from 5 pm to 1 am in her home office. She works for countries in different time zones that start and end their working day in these hours.

Additionally, know when it's right to take on a major task. For example, at the end of a school year, I was still wound up from the extraordinarily busy weeks of marking, reporting, etc. So, when school finished, I still had nervous energy that needed burning off. This was the optimum time to spring clean the office and help keep a more minimalistic workplace. I could then start my holidays relaxed, knowing everything was in order and ready for the following year.

Create a Timetable

The following timetable shows a manager having time at their desk punctuated by walking around the office or meeting with staff in the board room. Staff will then get to know the manager's routine. If the manager has a daily habit of moving around the staff each day just before lunch, they are less likely to have constant interruptions at their desk from staff at other times of the day. This could then leave them with blocks of time to accomplish solitary tasks. The manager may feel anxious until they have checked all their incoming mail, so it might be best to do that first thing. Late afternoon with the workplace buzzing might be the time to close the door and concentrate on report writing or analysis:

0900–1100	open mail, emails, write replies, and answer calls
1100–1115	meditate on your morning coffee
1115–1200	check-in with staff, e.g. issues (take diary to note points)
1200–1300	lunch and exercise
1300–1400	banking, bills, debtors, and ordering
1400–1500	meetings (afternoon tea included)
1500–1630	reports, analysis, and programming
1630–1700	tick off today's to do list, go over today's notes in diary from telephone calls/conversations, and write to do list for tomorrow (A4 size diaries with the week in view are excellent for keeping track of these notes).

This person is more likely to come home from work feeling satisfied with their day and be able to compartmentalise their work from home life. They know they have an attack plan (to do list) for tomorrow and have a sense of achievement by ticking off what they did today. Thus, they can come home clear-headed and ready to include some important meditation, which will only enhance their performance tomorrow!

Rise Earlier

An alternative to a time management plan to fit in meditation during a normal day is to rise thirty minutes earlier each morning. If one is meditating seriously every day, the meditation would more than compensate for the thirty minutes of lost sleep. I recall someone calculating that getting up thirty minutes early every day would add seven and a half years to the average life span. How wonderful to have an extra seven and half years of meditation, which would enhance all the other hours, days, and years of our life.

If you are getting up thirty minutes earlier, go to bed thirty minutes earlier to compensate. If you are tired when the alarm goes off, it could mean you just need time to adjust your body clock, so you might want to try waking ten minutes earlier for one week, then twenty minutes earlier the next, and thirty minutes earlier the final week. When starting the day earlier, we may wake with a state of mind that can be called 'the alien on your face'. You wake, and it is like an alien is saying, 'You shouldn't have to get up early; you deserve to go back to sleep.' And so it goes on and on, giving you excuses. Try to ignore this negative self-chatter, and just get out of bed before discussing the time with yourself!

Committing to a New Routine

It can take three weeks to cement a new routine in your life. During this period, you may have times of aversion to the new routine and make excuses, but if you can push through and maintain your commitment for twenty-one days, then the negative attitude will subside. Warn yourself that if you weaken during the first twenty-one days, you need to start counting twenty-one consecutive days again. Notice how much calmer and happier you are when you follow a routine. Recollect how flummoxed you got when running late and how often it can lead to accidents or mistakes. Embrace the commitment to be responsible and on time. Using a time management plan can certainly help to meet this achievement.

Morning routine

Time planning can be used for getting into a good morning routine, for example:

6.30 am   shower

6.45 am   relaxation and meditation (even fifteen minutes is better than none)

7.15 am   dress for work

7.30 am   coffee, breakfast, and make lunch

8.00 am   clean up dishes, make bed, clean teeth

8.30 am   leave for work.

Afternoon routine

Maybe there is no time for relaxation and meditation in the morning. You might even look at your life and consider there is no time in the afternoon or early evening. Look again! A busy household might start getting dinner ready at 5.30 pm, but this could be a time when the little ones under school age are particularly demanding. So, you could consider completely changing your routine to give you the time you are seeking to meditate daily. Here's an example:

5.30 pm   feed children (take from fridge and heat meal made night before)

6.00 pm   bath children

6.30 pm   bedtime story, settle, and sleep

7.00 pm   cook dinner but put children's dinner in fridge for the
           next night

8.00 pm   adults eat in peace

8.30 pm   meditation for thirty minutes

Sometimes chaos just takes a bit of planning to avoid. Think about how you could plan your weekday evenings. Planning your evening can help free up your weekend from home duties.

Friday housework routine

Do you get to the weekends and feel it's all about attending to the home? Then, before you know it, it is Monday, you are back at work, and you have not had a chance to rejuvenate.

I found a way around this. I would often spend Friday evenings having a drink with colleagues. Instead, we decided that I would come straight home from work and spend the three hours from 4 pm putting the washing on and hanging it out while attending to the vacuuming, washing floors, bathrooms, kitchen cleaning, etc. It was a great workout at the end of a week and a better way to burn off the stress than zonking out on alcohol.

My husband took the shopping list off the fridge on Friday mornings and would do all the shopping for the week, buy a takeaway dinner, and come home and pack away the shopping. By 7 pm, we would be settled in to watch a movie together, after having had a pizza with a glass of wine.

By setting up a system to take care of all the household jobs at one time and splitting the chores, you become much more proficient at doing them as you end up with a routine. If you do bits and pieces of jobs throughout the week, you can feel it's never-ending, for example you may end up washing the bathrooms too often or not vacuuming as often as needed.

Weekend freedom

At 7 pm on Friday nights, we had a wonderful sense that the main work was behind us, and we could have a restful and enjoyable weekend. As a result, we often would jump out of bed Saturday morning, energised from the sense this was our two days and head out to the beach. Sundays could be spent with friends and family, going out where we wanted, or chilling out at home.

Sunday evenings, I would do the ironing while my husband cooked the dinner. Thus, our weekends were largely our own to do as we pleased without a feeling of guilt over what we should have been doing and the working week was free of home pressures.

Weekly food plan

During those years, we had seven meals on our weekly menu that changed on a seasonal basis, for variety. We decided our favourite meals and would merely repeat these each week, for example one season we had: spaghetti bolognaise, fried rice, chicken and salad, beef curry, ham and salad, macaroni cheese with vegetables, steamed fish with vegetables. I set up an A4 page with all the ingredients needed for these seven meals, added other essentials to the list, and made photocopies of the original. Each week, I would go through the sheet and cross off any ingredients we already had in the pantry/fridge.

It might sound boring to have the same seven meals, but when these are your staples, you learn to cook them extremely well and quickly. The meals became restaurant standard. This took the pressure off when we were both working full time, undertaking tertiary studies, and raising a child.

Exercise 3—Time Management

1. Write a time management plan that includes a meditation session every morning.
2. Create a to-do list for the next day. Place a box next to each item to tick when completed. This gives a sense of achievement and pleasure. The list can be on your phone, on paper, or in your diary.

Meditation Difficulties

You may feel several sensations or experiences during the early sessions of meditation, which can be another difficulty or roadblock to meditating. Do not let these put you off but understand that what is happening is part of learning the practice.

Dropping sensation

When people start to meditate, they may experience a dropping or sinking sensation. It appears that as the mind becomes more peaceful, a sinking sensation results as you go inward to your centre. It is the break from the outside to the inside world. Some people experience this when they are slipping into sleep, the stepping down from the conscious to the unconscious mind.

However, in meditation, we aim to have both parts of the mind open and connected during this time. The dropping sensation might be pleasurable as you drop your attention to everything around you and welcome a more peaceful state within. Just go with any dropping or sinking sensation and allow it to happen. Concentrate on your breath, and the feeling will slowly subside. If it bothers you and you feel less in control, visualise yourself on a cushion of air allowing you to float to a more peaceful place. If you cannot picture a scene, then use words, such as 'a cushion of air is floating me to a more peaceful sense of being'.

Exhilarating sensation

Another sensation that is possible is the release of hyperactive tension. You may have had a hectic day, and this is the body's way of cleansing, releasing the energy. It may feel like a burst of energy, a buzz, or a feeling of total bliss. The mind can become bright and lead to rapture and joyous feelings in the body. This is a very pleasurable feeling, which comes from a concentrated mind. Just allow the body to experience this stage and try to maintain your attention on the breath.

Meditating When Tired

Another mistake or difficulty students encounter in the early stages is to undertake meditation when tired.

When I was pregnant with our son, my husband rushed in from work to the antenatal class. The beginning of the lesson was designed for the partner to help the mother-to-be learn how to relax. We all lay down in the prone position, listening to our instructor, and within a couple of minutes from beside me came heavy snoring. My husband was certainly relaxed!

People sometimes assume that if they are happy to sit down and watch an hour and a half movie, they could relax and meditate. Watching a movie is more of a mindless act and feeds our desire to be continually entertained and weakens the mind as it encourages us to wander in any direction.

If you know you are tired and could only sit in front of a screen, do not meditate. It would be better to do a little yoga exercise to restore the body's energy flow before meditating. A good yoga pose involves sitting next to the wall, with legs stretched out along the length of the wall. Then lie down on your back and swing the legs up the wall. Move your buttocks a little away from the wall if you feel a stretch, that is, if the muscle at the back of your legs is too tight. Move the shoulders a little to support the body and stay like that for a few minutes. You will find the pose rejuvenating, and this could also be carried out at work to give you a lift in the afternoon!

Quality Not Quantity

It is a mistake to conclude that the amount of time spent meditating is an indicator of your success. Many students ask me how much time they should spend each day or think they should meditate thirty minutes every day. Training the mind is difficult, and you may only be able to maintain a level of mindfulness for a few minutes or even just a few seconds in the early stages. Quality is what we are seeking, not quantity!

If you spend thirty minutes in what you think is meditation, but for twenty-eight of these minutes, you have thoughts coming in randomly, then you only achieved two minutes of concentrated focus on the breath. In the early stages, use the guided relaxation of the body session, which takes about twenty minutes to complete, then try to meditate for a further ten minutes.

The key to success is to have an interest in your meditation, be alert and awake in the present, watch the breath going in and going out. It requires you to be more than just conscious. Being conscious but not alert allows you to daydream. Most of the time, we are absent; we do not know that we are continually thinking, thinking, thinking. Where is your attention now? We can calm the storm in our mind and bring it to a tranquil pool where we have clarity of thought.

Constant Mental Chatter

Another early difficulty in meditation is our lack of awareness of how much the mind is caught up in constant chatter. You think you are not thinking, yet you are thinking about going to work and then thinking of work you must do when you get there, and so you have had a whole stream of thoughts. The moment in meditation that you wake up and become aware of the thinking is precious. Hold that quality; it is like an awakening. Hold that moment of stillness; that is what we are training the mind to do. To hold on to one thing at a time. Awareness and alertness are the key. It leads you to truth, insight, and wisdom that comes from a disciplined mind.

If you are having difficulty keeping the mind free of thoughts during the meditation session, the following technique may assist.

During the practical sessions, you have been shown how to focus on the breath, and as a thought comes push it aside gently but firmly. If thoughts continue to flood in, then use the Zen method of counting. Count the breath as it comes in and say 'one', then count the same breath going out and say 'one'. Continue this up to the number nine. If you a thought intrudes, start the breath again from one. For some time, you may not get beyond one or two before a thought will come in and have to start counting again. With time you will gain control over the mind and be rewarded. You will reach nine without a thought disturbing the stillness of the mind. Once you have overcome the random thoughts arising, try dropping the counting and return to observing the breath going in and out. Some days, the mind may be harder to settle than others, so reintroduce the counting whenever it is needed.

Imagery

Another problem is imagery while meditating. People can be distracted by constant mental chatter, but they can also be distracted by mental pictures. These pictures could be in the form of faces, objects, colours, patterns, and lights. As with constant chatter, it is just as important to maintain concentration on the breath. Imagery may be your mind wanting to play games, to entertain you in preference to being disciplined. The mind can be incredibly determined. It can side-track us from our mission to concentrate on the breath.

Should you experience distractions of imagery, just allow it to happen. Hold your attention on the breath, and all the faces, objects, colours, or lights will fade as you continue to focus on the breath. Do not be hard on yourself and disappointed when the images appear. Let them come and go without any attachment to them. That is, if an image of your partner comes in, do not start an inner conversation about that person. Stay detached, and just as the image has arisen, so shall it fall away. Maintain your concentration on the breath, and the images will have nothing to feed on.

Discomfort

Often during meditation, discomfort can distract us. Our lives are filled with avoiding pain while seeking pleasure and comfort. We crave stimulation and want our senses entertained or satisfied. We usually manage to fill our whole lives, so we never just sit and contemplate, reflect, or experience stillness.

It is little wonder that while sitting in meditation a student gets bored or sore and wants to move. It seems natural to us to want to fidget or move to end the discomfort from sitting in a certain position for a period. If you get bored, know that you decided to place a value on the experience as boring. No person or thing can make us bored. It is an emotion we choose, like the emotion to be happy or sad. You make the mental decision to be bored about the experience of peacefulness and stillness. Another person may decide to be joyous in the same experience. It is all up to your interpretation. So, gaining the knowledge that you create your own condition, choose to change it!

While sitting in meditation, it is important to cut off from the need for stimulation. For example, if you get an itch on your nose or a tingle in your big toe, know it, but that is all, do not attend to it. It is important to remain perfectly still during meditation. This does not mean that if a sitting creates excruciating pain that you ignore it. On the other hand, every little itch is an opportunity to strengthen the mind and stay true to the course. Stay focused on the breath. Maintain a perfectly still body as it is the pathway to the quest for stilling the mind.

The longer you meditate, the more you will find that when you are in the meditative state you lose sense of your body. It is a wonderful release to leave the body and only be in touch with the mind. It is possible after such a level of meditation to find you have, much to your surprise, a dead leg. I am certainly not indicating that you need to have pain to meditate well. I do not follow the practice of no pain, no gain; however, a slight discomfort such as an itchy nose could be welcomed as it helps the meditator develop concentration on the breath.

I use a meditative technique whenever I am having an injection. I relax my body and place my whole attention on my right big toe! Yes, as I focus on my right big toe, I cannot feel the needle going in. I wiggle my toe to keep my attention on the toe and away from the arm. If you are truly sensing your toe moving, you cannot feel anything happening in your upper arm. This is a great technique to teach children from a young age so that injections are never a problem.

Meditation gives you the ability to mentally detach from continually experiencing the body. It also gives you the ability to concentrate on the mind. Later you will learn how you can deeply concentrate on a certain area of the body to the exclusion of other parts.

Wakefulness

Some students of meditation complain that if they meditate at night, prior to going to bed, they are so alert and rejuvenated that they cannot settle to sleep. Therefore, some people may need to schedule their meditation time to occur during the day. Hence my suggestion for building it into one's early morning routine, giving you the alertness that will start your day in a positive and productive frame of mind. If you are unable to undertake meditation in the morning, the early afternoon or early evening when you first arrive home from work may be an alternative.

Practise is the Best Teacher

To overcome any problems or difficulties when meditating, the best advice is to continue to practise. Make a lifelong commitment to doing this every day, knowing it will be of great benefit to you, improving your quality of life.

Audio Practical Session 2: Meditation in the Sitting Position—Zen Counting

You are now ready to listen to the practical session available on the audio recording. Repeat this session many times over the week at a regular set time.

Session 3: Active Meditation

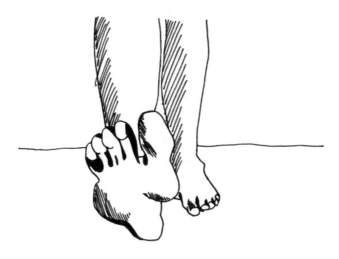

A young monk was given a broom to sweep the courtyard in front of the monastery. The senior monk visited him each day, and as he watched, he knew the young monk had not developed mindfulness. Day after day, the senior monk would shake his head as he walked past. Then one day, the senior monk smiled as he saw the young monk was making progress with disciplining his mind. How could he tell by merely observing the young monk sweeping?

In the early days, the senior monk noticed the novice sweeping all over the place. He would sweep a bit this way and then move and sweep in a different spot, changing direction. The breeze would blow some of his leaves, and he would tackle these and bring them back into a pile.

However, as time passed, the novice would start at one end and sweep with the breeze and in a straight line, easily gathering up more and more leaves as he went. The young *monk had learned to put his whole mind into the menial task. He had become more logical and efficient, completing the job in less time with a better outcome.*

Menial work carried out mindfully gives us the opportunity to discipline and train our minds for all aspects of our lives.

Sweeping in this fashion is one form of active meditation. Many chores can be used to practise this form of meditation. This session includes an exercise using a chore to complete active meditation and walking meditation, where your focus is on movement.

Setting aside a time of the day to undertake either prone position relaxation on the breath or a sitting position using Zen counting are two very formal methods of meditation. If you are an especially busy person, who finds it difficult to lie down or sit still, a more active form of meditation, such as walking meditation, might be the best place to start your journey towards a stiller, more disciplined mind. For those who have ADHD (the ultimate in busy minds), you might find walking meditation a particularly good exercise to introduce into your daily life and move to the prone and sitting meditations later.

Walking Meditation

Walking meditation involves walking in a certain, mindful manner. You cannot use your normal walk around the suburb as a method of walking meditation. You need to focus the mind on the subtle movements of your feet and legs and not be distracted by a passer-by or sightseeing when you are completing this walking meditation.

Find an area that will allow you to walk ten metres in a straight line before having to turn around and return along the ten metres. Find a quiet time when you will not be disturbed. Take off your shoes and socks so you are barefooted. Wear comfortable clothes. Use Practical Session 3 audio and follow the instructions for learning the skills of mindful walking.

This walk is not like your usual walk as it will focus on the subtle movements of your feet as you slowly place the heel then the instep, and finally your toes on the path before lifting your other foot and doing the same. This extremely slow, mindful walking triggers the mind to slow down in unison with the movement of the feet.

The experience is more beautiful if undertaken outside in the fresh air and nature. You may have seen priests walking a set garden path as they say the Rosary. Here the slow body movement allows the mind to settle and concentrate on the repetition of the Rosary verses. In this audio practice, your concentration will be on the repetition of the movement of your feet.

I have a clear memory of the first time a monk took me through the walking meditation. It was about 6 am in the hills of Perth. The scene was beautiful, fresh air, a chilly clear morning, the ground was moist, the birds singing, and the area filled with people having chosen their ten paces of ground. I looked around and could see everyone walking extremely slowly back and forth. It was so cold being winter, yet the monk was only in his robe and sandals. How did he not feel the cold? As I focused on my step ... heel ... instep ... toes and I found the cold was an outside thing I could detach from. I honed in on my steps, and even the bird's songs disappeared as I focused on the sensation of my step by step moving across the ground.

Find your own special place to walk. Choose somewhere that has a ten-metre distance that you can pace, for example, the back lawn or courtyard. It would be ideal if there was a straight, flat path in your garden. You might like to create one by laying a short, straight concrete path. It must not wind through a garden as you need to be able to automatically traverse the path back and forth, maintaining your focus on the subtle movements of your body.

On some days, the mind can be more difficult to settle, and walking meditation might be a great alternative to prone breathing or sitting counting. This could be especially true during busy workdays.

Find a room at work where you can go to complete mindful walking for fifteen minutes during your lunch break.

Walking mindfulness is also a joy to undertake on holidays in the countryside or at the beach (on wet, hard sand). This can be a daily session to raise your awareness and be more alert to the joys of rejuvenation that come from being in nature.

Use your phone to scan the QR code for access to the audio music and guided session that is included with this book. This will help raise your productivity level in the afternoon due to the reinvigoration effect this technique has on the mind and body.

As mentioned at the outset of this session, mindfulness can be undertaken while carrying out everything in your day. Initially, this could be exhausting because you are not used to it, so choose a menial task, such as washing the dishes, to develop the skill. That is, give your total attention to the job at hand. Try the following tonight.

Exercise 4—Chores

1. Observe yourself placing the plug in the sink, filling the sink with water, and adding the detergent.
2. Feel the texture of the water as you move your hands in the warm water to wash the dishes.
3. Take an interest in every morsel of food you are removing from the dishes.
4. Do not allow thoughts to come in, do not daydream. Stay gently and firmly focused on the task at hand.
5. Notice that washing the dishes cannot be something you dislike if you stay mindful. This is because you are not allowing yourself to make a value judgement.
6. Notice how refreshed you feel because you have stopped the exhausting constant chatter of your mind.
7. See how the dishes sparkle as every job carried out in this matter will be of superior quality!

In time, you will come to have a trained mind so that when given a mountainous problem, you will be able to bring a superior level of concentration and wisdom to the problem. Additionally, when you are training the mind, there is a tendency to be more disciplined when going about your normal day's activities.

Audio Practical Session 3: Walking With Focus

You are now ready to listen to the practical session available on the audio recording. Repeat this session many times over the week.

Session 4: Reducing Stress

Stress

Relax

As you carry out this session, you will need to have the following at your disposal:

- one glass of water
- toothpaste and toothbrush
- peaceful background music (nature, classical piano, or flute)
- an array of foods you really enjoy
- incense or oil burner
- flowers.

Drink

Before we start, drink half the glass of water. Do not read on until you have carried out this first instruction.

******

How much notice did you take when drinking the water? You probably were thinking, *Why on earth do I need to drink half a glass of water?* or *What is the point of this exercise?* This is to show that when we carry out daily routines, we are rarely present. We are in the future or past but not present to our moment in time. We are worrying over the bills that must be paid or fussing over a disagreement we had earlier in the day. Our mind is preoccupied, and whenever it is behaving in this monkey mind way, we are not living in the present. If we are thinking about why we were asked to drink the water while we were drinking the water, then we were not actually drinking the water!

Now finish the glass of water, but this time be only with the act of drinking. Be at one with your body while it is drinking. Notice any sensations to the lips, the effect on the tongue, the sliding of the water past your throat. Did you notice the water has a smooth texture and that it was cool to your throat?

Imagine if you took this much notice of the cuppa you have each morning to start your day. This is one way you can reduce stress in your body each day. Make a promise to yourself that the first cup of the day, or the first cuppa when you arrive home from work, is consumed in a peaceful setting. Be alone, where you can really experience the drink. If you live in an apartment, then maybe look forward to doing this en route to work or from work by stopping off at a park with a takeaway cuppa.

Exercise 5—Cuppa Break

1. Sit quietly with your cuppa.
2. Like the mindfulness on the glass of water, the mindfulness on the cuppa is much the same.

3. Notice the effect on your lips, tongue, and gums as the drink enters your mouth.
4. Notice the smoothness of the liquid, the temperature, the taste, and feel it flowing down your throat.
5. Drink slowly, and as any thoughts come in, see your hand in your mind's eye, gently pushing your thoughts away so that you remain at one with the drinking.

Memory of an Experience

We have probably all heard someone say, 'I could kill for a cuppa'. Somehow, we expect a hot drink to soothe, relax us, and ease the stresses of the day. However, most of us can drink while walking around the house getting ready, answering the phone, or talking to a friend. Most of us are doing or thinking of something else while we have what we think is a special cuppa.

I believe the cuppa triggers the brain to relax, based on our first memories of what it did for us (plus the chemical reaction that stimulates the brain from coffee/tea). Have you noticed that when you first try a new food or drink, you stop talking and concentrate on the experience? You might play around with the food in your mouth and chew it slowly to ensure you experience the flavours. We no doubt did that with our first cup of tea or coffee. We enjoyed the relaxed moment, yet for much of the rest of our life, we rely on the memory of that first experience to enjoy future cuppas. We do not have time to re-experience and be fully present in the moment. We are not prepared to stop and enjoy the total experience each time we have a cuppa.

How about taking the time, each time? The above exercise, if completed daily, will be a time to reconnect, if only for a few minutes, to rejuvenate and enjoy a space in the moment of being at one with your mind and body.

Ablutions

Can you recall a day when you rushed off to work and wondered later if you brushed your teeth? How many of us are away with the birds while we are brushing our teeth? You may have been thinking, *Oh no, I'm late for work!* or *Will the traffic be slow this morning?*

Again, we are not living in the present. We are not taking every opportunity to train the mind to act as a tool for thinking and solving problems; instead, we have become slaves to the erratic thought processes that continually exhaust us.

It would be beneficial to use the time taken to clean our teeth to practise mindfulness. By thinking about being late for work, you are not going to change the reality of probably being late. So instead of stressing, you might as well calm down, so when you arrive late you can immediately function productively.

Teeth cleaning mindfulness is wonderful to introduce to children, so they can start to train their minds at an early age. Parents/ guardians can talk them through the technique prior to going to bed. You could even purchase a timer to sit on your bathroom bench and set the timer for two minutes. Your dentist will thank you!

This is an easy way to train your mind to be disciplined and not dart off here and there. This can be two minutes of mind training every morning and evening and adds no more time to your everyday routine. It is another way you can reduce stress in your body daily. Make a promise to yourself that every evening at least, when you clean your teeth, you will complete the task with mindfulness to help create a calm, peaceful state within.

Exercise 6—Cleaning Teeth

1. In the bathroom, be mindful from the moment you pick up the toothpaste and toothbrush.
2. Observe yourself placing the toothpaste on the toothbrush.

3. If a thought comes to mind, allow it to wash over you, do not entertain it. For example, if you think, *I forgot to do such and such yesterday.*
4. Avoid acknowledging the thought and adding fuel to the fire by continuing thoughts such as, *I hope no one notices what I missed.*
5. Bring the attention back to the toothbrush and toothpaste.
6. Taking the brush to your mouth, begin to clean your teeth, observing the effect on your mouth.
7. Feel the brush going round and round on the teeth. Feel the brush moving over your gums.
8. Notice the taste, texture, and temperature of the toothpaste in your mouth.
9. Feel the water swirling around your mouth as you rinse.

Backdrops to Your Life

Have you ever noticed when you have an assignment/report due, you suddenly need to clean the house? You may say this is procrastination and feel bad about your inability to start the work report or student assignment. Sometimes it may be procrastination, but it could also be your inner core screaming out for some sort of order. Just like your mind needs to be uncluttered, sorted, and ordered, so does the backdrop for the place you complete your work and carry out your personal life.

Possessions can weigh us down

Do you work at a desk? What does it look like? Do you waste time looking for things because there is no order or system? Is your kitchen the same? When you want to find something to wear, do you hunt through the mess, wondering whether it is clean or dirty? Are your work place and home full of clutter? Do your possessions own you?

Happiness is about having a meaningful life. Material possessions do not necessarily make us happy; they just weigh us down. People have stuff they must cart around, and when they get too much stuff, they hire a storage unit!

At the Buddhist Jungle Monastery in Thailand, it was inspiring to see each monk had their own living quarters. These were sprinkled throughout the grounds of the monastery. Each monk reached his abode by climbing a ladder, as it was off the ground at about head height. The units looked more like kid's cubbies than bedrooms. They had openings but no windows or doors. Each timber box-type dwelling was about the size of two single beds in width and length. The monks each had robes, sandals, personal hygiene items, a food bowl, a carry sling bag, and little else. Yet they were happy!

Desire creates more desires

People can get caught up in the endless, never satisfied desire addiction. Perhaps you have just bought a new car, but soon you will desire something better, the next model up. And so, we go on striving for material possessions, buying to fill in our time and an emotional void. Instead, we could stop, take stock, and decide what we really need to have a happy life.

Try committing to a month of not buying anything other than the food you need and see how this calms the endless desire addiction. We even buy too much food. 'On average, we Australians throw one in five shopping bags of food in the bin – that's about $3,800 worth of groceries per household each year.'[5] Writing up a quick menu of meals for the week before doing the shopping will prevent wastage.

Put some of the money saved from only buying essentials for that month into a savings account and maybe give a little to charity. See how this makes you feel over time by only buying essentials. Initially, maybe

5 https://www.foodbank.org.au/food-waste-facts-in-australia/?state=nsw-act

commit to every second month when you will only buy essentials so that you gradually raise your awareness of conscious consumerism. I heard recently that many people live from week to week. That's not a way to feel secure. So, build up your savings for life's surprises! A little at a time will add up if you don't touch it except for emergencies. Having a surplus reduces stress and gives you choices.

Money doesn't equal happiness

I read about a multi-millionaire who committed suicide, which supports the idea that possessions and money do not guarantee happiness. So, saying to yourself, 'When I have X, I will be genuinely happy,' is just not true. Having a constant state of unhappiness and discontent happens slowly over time. Years and years of dissatisfaction gradually eat away at our joy. You may find that you, or some of your friends, are in the same situation, unaware of the rot that has set in.

Gross National Product or Gross National Happiness?

When I was lecturing for the University of Sydney on their Orange campus, I met a student from Bhutan. He was doing a short course in rural management research. I was living on campus in a villa, and he was in the halls of residence, but we both used the same cafeteria. One evening, he and I were in the dining area, and we sat together and chatted. Having completed an economic degree as an undergraduate, I was keen to talk to him about the difference between Australia's GNP and Bhutan's GNH.

I was aware that Australia and many western parts of the world measure their nation's success by Gross National Product (GNP). Our government gauge our success in terms of economic growth. The western world, with its ever-growing economies, has issues with pollution, social discord, increasing gap between the rich and poor, and deforestation, to name but a few negative outcomes of our ever-increasing growth in production seeking profit.

The Bhutanese man explained how their measure of achievement is measured by a Gross National Happiness (GNH). This comes from information gathered from the population reporting on their current level of happiness. Their aim is to keep incomes of the country rising but without sacrificing the overall wellbeing of the people of the nation. The king, Jigme Singye Wangchuk, set about promoting self-reliance and progress, but the king was determined to underpin this with the principles of good governance, inclusive development, conservation, and preservation of Bhutan's culture.

The student went on to say that they do not evaluate their worth by an ever-increasing standard of living shown by a dollar value. He felt this was a flawed approach in the West, and we agreed there is an ever-widening gap between the haves and the have-nots, which we both found disturbing. In the West, we have a higher average level of wealth in dollar values, but this is a skewed result because billionaires are becoming trillionaires while others move to live below the poverty line. I thought Bhutan's idea to measure wealth in terms of the happiness of the nation's inhabitants had merit.

He stressed that we equate our nation's happiness to our economic wealth but reminded me there is an important balance between material and non-material wealth, including cultural aspects of our lives. We would do well to undertake the same measure of happiness using set criteria to see if happiness is increasing or, as I suspect, declining in this very materialist, profit-driven economy. It seems to me that progress at this moment doesn't place value on the principles of good governance, inclusive development, conservation, and preservation of our multicultural nation.

Conscious Consumerism

If Bhutan can change its focus to something more soulful than economic, why can't we do the same? Maybe we could start with people's mindless expenditures? We can all become conscious consumers and stop buying things that end up as landfill. Do not blame yourself too much or feel overwhelmed by how much needs improving in our world. Do your bit, and you may be surprised at how this generation is evolving; eventually, there will be a tipping point where the minority value becomes a majority held value.

In this century, we are bombarded every waking hour with advertisements and the pressure to buy, buy, buy things we do not need. So, make a commitment to avoid advertising any way that you can. For example, avoid the shopping channel and commercial television stations, make a conscious effort not to disturb your world by reading signs and billboards, do not give your email address or mobile phone number to any shops. Do not follow influencers who promote unconscious consumerism. Think of ways you could stop the endless stream of pressure to purchase more things that will not promote your happiness or stillness of mind. Be the start of values of conscious consumerism held by the minority becoming values held by the majority.

Declutter

What will help you be happy is to sort out the places you live and work. Even if this means going in to work for a full weekend to clear out mess and make some order, it might be what you need to do for your improved well-being. Your home may be chaotic with stuff everywhere, but you can start small with the easiest area to cleanse. This way you will have a sense of achievement that can be built on over time when you tackle more difficult areas. Maybe just start with your wardrobe.

I started by standing in front of my wardrobe equipped with two huge different coloured plastic bags. One was for the things I was about to throw out (black) and the other for charity (white). I then took out one item at a time, as I felt holding each item was an important way to engage all my senses and stay focused. It prevented becoming distracted and only giving a cursory glance to the clothing. I took out the first item, which was a pair of long pants. I examined them and asked myself if I had worn them in the past year. No! So, it would be kinder to let the trousers go. Otherwise, it just becomes stuff I must find a place to store. I placed the trousers into the white bag.

I examined the other items one by one. If something was in disrepair, and no one could benefit from it, I placed it in the black bag. If the item was in good condition, it was kinder for me to pass the item on to charity, so I popped it in the white bag. I said to myself, *What I do not need will help someone else in need!* In this way, I calmed myself to be willing to let it go and reminded myself it creates good karma. It is not good karma to place all the items you don't want into the white bag and take it to charity. If it is junk, it is your responsibility to dispose of it by placing it in your own rubbish bin. Dirty or damaged items can't be resold in the charity shops, but they may be bundled up as rags, and unfortunately are sometimes sold to Indonesia as clothing. This is because buyers from Indonesia must buy a bag without seeing inside and hope what they get are marketable items. Recently, a documentary showed these poor-quality items often end up in piles as big as houses at the end of a village where they are burned, creating a breathing hazard for the villagers.

Once the black bag was full, I immediately placed it in the bin, and I drove the white bag to the closest charity bin (found at most shopping centres). I did not put the white bag in the garage for fear I would slowly return the items to the wardrobe, or they would remain forever as junk in my garage. When I finished the cleansing, I felt a sense of freedom, uncluttered, a release from the things weighing me down.

At the end of sorting my wardrobe, I revelled in the space I created. Just like one's mind, with less clutter, more clarity arises. Once I reduced the number of things in my wardrobe, I put the clothing into groups: trousers, tops, jackets, etc. Now when I'm looking for a particular top, I do not have to go through everything I own, I can just check the tops that are all hanging together. I did the same things with my underwear, t-shirts, bras, socks, etc. I find it easier to keep things in order and that is a great backdrop to help me feel more in control of my life.

If you decide to take up the challenge, remember when you finish to go out and celebrate. Mark your achievements. Reward yourself for carrying out such a goal. To help with motivation, you could tell your friends what you have planned. They might want to do the same thing, so set up a morning to commit to cleansing your wardrobe and arrange to meet for lunch to talk about the freeing experience that you have gained from minimising.

Less is More

Minimalism in the western world started in the 1950s and 1960s in the areas of art, design, and music. It was a mixed artistic movement and evolved. However, it started far earlier in the East, where minimalism dates back thousands of years and is all about creating a holistic clutter-free environment in which to live simply. For example, Zen gardens show structure, sparseness, and order. Buddhist monks have lived with sparseness all their lives as part of the search for enlightenment.

I learned the mantra 'less is more' from a friend. I was getting dressed to go out on a date and asked him if he thought my earrings and necklace were a bit much together. My friend just answered,

'Less is more'. It was a light bulb moment for me as I quickly removed the gaudy earrings that were in fashion at the time but were so over the top. I now use this mantra often to fine-tune what is important. The trivial fade away as I keep things simple, and I have learned that beauty comes from less.

Start with your home and make it the greatest support system for you. Then move on to your work. How can you make your home and workplace like a beautiful Zen garden where there is only what you need with a plant or two to soften and create a harmonious environment?

We can become conscious consumers limiting our purchases to the essentials, and by reducing, reusing, and recycling, we can help our planet too. Find other ways than shopping to enjoy your life and awaken what is important in life. Giving a morning to help a charity could be a start. When you next buy a birthday present for a friend, think about it consciously and consider purchasing an experience instead of adding to their stuff. A voucher for local movies or lunch, a massage, or a facial is a great idea, and staying local means using fewer fossil fuels that diminish the planet's resources.

How Much Do We Need?

A popular minimalist is Colin Wright, who set up *Exile Lifestyle* at twenty-four years of age. He mindfully selected seventy-two items to support his life while he travelled the world, allowing him to focus on the important stuff in his life and shed the excess junk that got in his way. I certainly could not get my belongings down to seventy-two items but knowing it can be done inspires me.

Some years ago, I helped a Rotary group with a pilot program to bring young people from Bali to Australia to give them skills and enhance their ability to provide for their families. In return, the young person joined the Indonesian language classes at the local school to help the students develop conversational language and inspire them to learn about the culture.

As a business teacher, I knew I could teach a great deal about working in an office as an administrator. Gede lived with us for three months, and I taught him after hours and gave him lessons at school during my periods off.

At our home, Gede was astounded at the number of t-shirts my son owned. He was astounded at our kitchen size and appliances. Gede explained that he only had a tin shack as a home and they cooked outside under what could best be described as a carport with a mini wood stove. They walked to the nearby markets where they bought all the food they needed in handmade containers, fed their scraps to the chickens, and buried the rest onsite.

Gede returned to Bali, and instead of earning a small wage as a gardener, he became the administrator of an eye clinic and was able to provide for his family. We learned a lot from one another over those three months. He learned about administration, and I had a chance to really evaluate my life's possessions.

Practise Each Day

Cleaning out your wardrobe can be a mindful exercise. You need to focus and stay with the task at hand. If cleaning your whole wardrobe seems like too much, break it up into separate sessions. For example, on day one, sort out your underwear drawer, on day two, your shirts, and so on. The ability to develop mindfulness can be carried out every day through your daily chores. Undertaking these tasks in a mindful fashion will help develop a clear mind and give rise to wisdom. The trained mind is far superior to the monkey mind and will be a tool to enhance your whole life experience.

If you have two cuppas each day and clean your teeth twice per day, then you could be using twenty minutes each day to develop mindfulness. If you are going through a particularly difficult time and are unable to find the time to formally meditate in the prone, sitting, or walking positions, you can still develop a disciplined mind and enjoy the sense of being mentally calm by mindfully completing menial tasks.

Meals

Do you eat your dinner in front of the television, gulping your food, hardly aware of what you are consuming? One of my adult students was terribly distressed about this. She would spend an hour or more preparing and cooking the evening meal, only to have it bolted down by the family. They seemed unaware of what they were eating, totally engrossed in television.

When people are faced with an array of desserts or a smorgasbord, they may see how much they can fit on their plate, rather than ask which one they would most like. We tend to give in to our desire and let this rule our thinking.

These are examples of not being present. If we were in touch with our senses and in tune with the present moment, we would realise the body would be satisfied with just one of the desserts. Eating in front of the television or screen distracts us from experiencing the sensations of eating the meal. We are not in touch with our bodies to know when we have had enough.

Most families spend time away from one another during the working week and so it is important to have time to maintain the bond and communicate through sharing time together each day.

As a director of upper high school, I was disturbed to find deeply wounded teenagers whose families were too busy to talk, share a meal, share meaningful times, and had lost communication skills and their connection to one another. I believe that a family that eats together is more likely to stay together. I have treasured memories of Saturday lunches at my parents-in-law's, where all the family descended to catch up each week. Making traditions like this set your children up to experience the enjoyment of rituals, especially where the whole family, all the generations, share time together.

Some years ago, I went on a meditation retreat. On my arrival, I was made aware that the participants were not allowed to speak the entire weekend. It was such an amazing experience to eat every meal over the weekend in a hall with dozens of other people who were not speaking. At first, I had a million thoughts coming in, *What if my friends could see me now, how they would laugh!*

As the weekend progressed, I began to notice what I was eating. There was a joy to be had in focusing all my attention on the food. Some of those meals were the best I have ever tasted. In fact, it has been shown that noisy backgrounds actually affect our tastebuds' ability to taste. I had never felt every morsel more clearly, noticed every flavour, or eaten a meal so slowly. When one is truly concentrating, you become more aware of what you are doing and far less likely to gulp. It was an opportunity to chew properly (I challenged myself to chew each piece for twenty seconds) and took breaks between mouthfuls to savour the flavour and experience.

The nearness to others at the table was also apparent. They were complete strangers but we developed a closeness as we sat opposite one another and side by side, sharing the experience. There was a significant connection between the people that did not involve conversation.

Eating in this way is a way of stilling the mind through being mindful and present. Here the food was the meditation object, instead of the breath during the prone position, or Zen counting in the sitting position, or the sensations of the feet during the walking meditation.

I am not suggesting the family needs to eat their meals eating mindfully in silence every night. However, it could be a wonderful one-off experience for the whole family and something they might like to repeat from time to time.

When you are alone is a great opportunity to undertake such an exercise.

Exercise 7—Eating Mindfully

1. Place an array of your favourite foods on the table. Sit alone in front of these foods.
2. Take one piece of food at a time and eat mindfully.
3. Notice the sound made when you are eating; some foods are crunchy, others melt in your mouth.
4. Notice the texture of the different foods you are choosing; some are smooth, others are rough.
5. Notice the temperature of the food and the sensation around and inside your mouth.
6. Maintain your full attention on the food. As a thought comes in, gently but firmly push it aside and return your attention to the mouthful of food being eaten.
7. Aim to chew each piece of food for twenty seconds. Rest between mouthfuls.

Take this eating mindfully one step further by involving the entire household in an evening meal where they agree not to talk. Complete the exercise I have described above as a group. Explain that speaking should only occur during this exercise to be polite, for example, 'Please pass the bread'. This is where noble silence prevails. No idle chatter or heavy discussion is undertaken. At the end of the meal, the group could discuss the experience.

Reducing Stress Through More Daily Practices

Even if you only eat your breakfast each day in noble silence, you would be developing your mindfulness skills for maybe fifteen minutes per day. Couple this with having a cuppa and cleaning your teeth mindfully; you would be mindful for thirty-five minutes per day. Thus, half an hour or more per day could be spent training your mind to be more disciplined and less stressed by keeping your attention on these chores that you must undertake anyway. There is no more time needed to be set aside to ensure a minimum of half an hour of daily mindfulness.

Sexual Intimacy

During sexual intimacy, it is unlikely that thoughts associated with work and other problems enter the mind. Sexual intimacy can be consuming, ensuring the person is present. It can be a great release of tension. The meditative focus is on the body and the pleasure brought to one another. It is a time of experiencing alertness—awakening one to the present moment. With such focus on the experience, to the exclusion of the outside world and thoughts, sexual intimacy is a form of meditation.

Tantric sex refers to a wide range of Hindu and Buddhist sexual yoga practices. These practices were developed to intimately connect one's spirituality and sexuality with a focus on feelings, senses, and shared connection during intimacy. Tantric techniques, such as gentle stroking, caressing, and creating a beautiful space with scented candles, ritualise the deep connection with one another in a meaningful way. Thus, a highly sensual, blissful, and spiritual experience unfolds. Tantric techniques lead to arousing sexual energy, creating sacred sexual fulfilment, and lovemaking, including prolonging and heightening pleasure and intimacy.

If you would like to learn more about Tantric sex, read *Tantric Sex: Step-by-Step Guide to Learning the Art of Tantric Sex* by Jim Owens and Grace Mason. If you want to improve your intimacy and develop your ability to pleasure one another, Tantric sex could take you beyond gaining physical skills to making a deep emotional and spiritual connection with your partner. However, if you do not wish to plunge into Tantric sex but want to improve your lovemaking and enhance your ability to be present and mindful, you might be interested in *The Ultimate Sex Book* by Anne Hooper.

As sex is no longer a taboo subject, families are seeing the benefits of discussing sex with their children. With most of the millennial generation embracing the sex culture, there has been a dramatic increase in the quantity of sex. However, amid the COVID-19 pandemic, attention has been drawn to the subject of porn, with pornography viewing reaching excessive levels and children as young as eight years of age accessing it. Teenagers with hormones raging and little or no experience explore the internet and may access porn. In some cases, eighteen-year-old boys are admitting they are addicted to pornography. However, to shame and criticise youth is not productive. It is important for teenagers to hear from their parents about sex and the truth about porn.

Youth may be ill-informed about sex by their friends, films, computer games, and porn, and they are exposed to visions of toxic masculinity that is indicative of aggression, privilege, and ownership. They are misinformed by social media platforms where some users and influencers can be seen to promote themselves as pawns in their partner's sexual desires. Sometimes the sensitive, caring person seems lost in the skewed versions of human contact promoted on the internet.

Society can mislead youth to think sex is the pinnacle of life. If it is, one's life becomes dysfunctional, with lust a never-ending illusion of desire. The need to 'score' creates an empty life of forever grasping and needing, trying to fill an empty cup. If one is caught up in this, it can take time to change the habit of seeking a quick fix instead of a meaningful relationship.

To change, the journey starts with not entertaining the negative thoughts that seek a short term high instead of a satisfying relationship. Disciplining the monkey mind with its impulses and endless desires gives one respect for oneself and others. This is all part of the pathway to sublime intimacy.

Focusing on becoming a respectful, responsible, caring, and dignified adult is highly successful in creating an emotionally mature adult. Behaving and treating others in a way you are proud of is part of the process of growing into the adult version of yourself. From this place, you will feel a radiance of inner confidence being in sync with your authentic, loving, sensual soul.

Hobbies

Have you ever noticed how the outside world fades when you are caught up doing something you enjoy? People become quite joyous and light while involved in a hobby they love. When the activity is over, there is a sense of renewal and one is ready to face the world again. The mind that is intensely interested finds it easy to focus, and we can lose our sense of time when engrossed in a hobby. I became acutely aware of the benefits of a hobby while voluntarily teaching overseas students ballroom dancing in the halls of residence at Monash University in Melbourne.

I noticed that even when starting the lesson and learning the first few steps, smiles would quickly blossom and laughter would fill the room. There is such a stress release from undertaking a hobby such as this. While the students were learning new steps, they had to concentrate. Concentration requires a single-minded approach that is necessary during meditation.

While dancing, they did not think about home or work life; they were there at that precise moment, living the reality of the moment. Not in the past or future, but in the present, step by step, glide by glide.

Not only did the students leave dancing each week happy, but I always came away from these sessions with a great sense of elation.

I'm sure some of this was the joy from moving to the music, but also from the feeling of giving back to one's community and sharing with others.

Any hobby has the potential to encourage the mind to concentrate and give it the rest and refresh it needs. It is a way of disciplining the mind on the activity, step by step, just like concentrating on the breath. When involved in a hobby or a sport, a person is being mindful.

Exercise 8—Hobbies/Sport to Evoke Mindfulness

Complete either 1 or 2 below:
1. If you currently have a hobby:
    a. Write down a few lines describing your hobby.
    b. How does your hobby make you feel?
    c. What is it about the hobby that keeps you engaged and coming back?
2. If you don't currently have a hobby, take a moment to seek inspiration:
    a. What hobbies did you have as a child?
    b. Can any of them translate into an adult activity?
    c. Try a couple on for size.
    d. Choose one that will let you switch off from your day.

Music

When the mind is operating too fast for long periods, it can be stressful. During this time of accelerated brain activity, you are probably operating on beta waves. The brain is not particularly good at problem-solving while it is working in this mode. We all have experienced this state of frenzy when our brain is not thinking clearly. It has been shown that the brain operates at its most efficient and productive level when producing alpha waves. When we summon a state of mind using alpha waves, we have a calmer, clearer way of looking at things.

So, in our hectic lives, we could be cooking dinner and worrying about a problem in our life. We are distracted from cooking and not focused on dinner. Hence, as a result, a burnt dinner and an unsatisfactory solution to our life problem. Instead, what if you had focused all your efforts on cooking the dinner, thus disciplining the mind, then after dinner sitting down and contemplating the problem?

You may have noticed that extremely calm people are often also gifted with incredible wisdom and seem to have a joyful approach to life. It is no coincidence that these attributes are found together.

Once we have learned to train the mind through mindfulness and meditation, and reduce erratic thought patterns changing from beta to alpha waves, then we have significantly increased our ability to think effectively. Meditation takes one from beta to alpha waves through focusing on the breath, counting, sensations, or whatever is the subject of our pointed attention.

How does music relate to all this? Peaceful music, such as piano, harp, pan flutes, or string instrumentals can provide the change from beta to alpha wave functioning of the brain and calm the mind. If you like more natural sounds, a mixture of bells, babbling brooks, whale songs, birds singing, or ocean waves might better suit your purpose. There is a wealth of relaxation music available today. The audio sessions accompanying this book use Tony O'Connor's array of music, or you could subscribe to your favourite streaming platform and create a playlist. Consider introducing such music at work to add a more tranquil background and block out office noise.

Some years ago, I designed, built, and operated a boutique childcare centre. The four staff and I each had a work vehicle and would pick up four or five children each morning from home and drop them back at the end of the day. One Friday afternoon, Harry's mum was there to greet me, and she reminded Harry to ask me about my favourite song. After a moment of deciding, I told him, and his mum explained that each Friday night a member of the family would play someone's choice of music. That week Harry wanted to play mine. A family ritual of playing music and dancing together is a wonderful way for children to experience and appreciate a wide variety of music.

Exercise 9—Music Relaxation

Complete either 1 or 2 below:

1. If you share a home with children:
   a. Make a time each day to listen to relaxation music or have it playing in the background. The stress will melt away.
   b. Early evening is normally a chaotic time. Young children are tired and hungry and the adults are busy getting dinner ready. Introduce some calming relaxation music to play quietly in the background.
   c. Have one parent bath the children and the other cook the meal. Children will thus get the attention and comfort they need from one parent, and the other parent can get dinner ready without interruptions.
2. If you share a home without children:
   a. When you return from work lacking in energy, this is the time to make a cuppa.
   b. Sit out in the garden or stop at a park on your way home from work and have some relaxation music playing in the background.

Flow On Effect

All the above-mentioned activities and exercises have a flow on effect on your quality of life. Being mindful when you are having your first cuppa, eating your breakfast, cleaning your teeth, listening to relaxation music, and undertaking a hobby are wonderful ways to reduce stress and create a calmer, more peaceful and content you. The more you train the mind to focus, the more likely your mind is to behave in this way at all other times of your day. If you continue to practise daily, you will increase the quality and length of time you have this heightened state of the mind. Mindfulness will become a way of being!

When mindfulness starts to be a way of being, you will find solutions to problems appear far easier and quicker. You will have improved conversations with others due to your increased ability to clearly listen. You may find you have fewer problems in your life due to your ability to deal with little things as they surface, and thus nip them in the bud before they develop into larger problems.

Problem Solving Through Visualisation

In this session's audio practical session, I will help you develop the art of creative visualisation to bring about a relaxed state. You will begin to allow your inner self to find peace by identifying possible solutions to your problems.

I will first take you through an exercise that guides you into a relaxed state where you will gradually let go of any tension. You will then enter a garden of your creation in your mind's eye. This is a wonderful opportunity to immerse yourself in a beautiful garden that you can visit anytime you want. If you live in a multi-level apartment, this is your access to your own Shangri-La (a fictional utopia—a mystical, earthly paradise with enduring happiness and almost immortal life in an isolated, harmonious valley in the Himalayas). If you have a garden or courtyard, creating this in your mind's eye can still be your place to go. Leave the problems of the world behind when you enter this relaxation exercise. Here you can ponder any problem and seek answers from your subconscious mind.

How often do people really take refuge in their garden? They are too busy weeding or mowing instead of sitting peacefully and appreciating their garden. How often are you stopped by a butterfly and follow its path as it flutters around your garden? Do you know your local butterfly? Do you know they only live for a few weeks and are quite territorial? If you see some beautiful wings today, you will only get the chance to see them again for the next few weeks. Will you make the time to appreciate nature and its wonders? We seem to have lost touch with the harmony of being at one with nature. It is time to reset the balance. How often do you stop to smell the roses?

Japanese Zen gardens are certainly inspirational. They have a beauty and symmetry and emanate a sense of peace. They are an ideal setting for practising meditation. The focal point in a Zen garden is usually a large rock framed by a fence, shrubs, potted plants, or some other barrier to separate it from the wider surroundings, creating a special quiet place for you to retreat. In the foreground is gravel with carefully placed plants. It is important that when the person enters the garden, they lose connection with the outside and this becomes their inner sanctum. Wind chimes or water can add atmosphere and help to calm the mind.

If you are not into the simplicity of a Zen garden, you might like to investigate Ellis Stone's book, *Australian Garden Design*. Ellis Stone was a landscape architect and the father of Australia's natural bush landscape style. He designed many public gardens and taught basic understanding, such as always placing the water at the bottom of the landfall, grouping trees in odd numbers, with five being ideal to give a clumping effect and mimicking what is found in nature.

Audio Practical Session 4: Garden Messages

You are now ready to listen to the practical session available on the audio recording. Repeat this session many times over the week at a set time.

Session 5: Creative Visualisation

A PICTURE IS WORTH A THOUSAND WORDS

C reative visualisation allows one to use mental imagery to bring about positive change in one's life. It is about using our imagination as we did as children. When we closed our eyes and daydreamed of being a princess or a prince, heroine or hero, we were entering the world of creative imagery. Some of us find it easy to use our imagination to bring pictures into our mind's eye, making mental images of what we are thinking about. This technique is used by elite athletes who are more likely to succeed if they visualise success; for example, a basketballer will stand in front of the ring and visualise the ball going in before they shoot.

For some people, mental imagery is more difficult to create. If this is the case for you, do not be discouraged. If you cannot see the images, then think about words that would be associated with the image. So, if you are thinking about being successful at your next job interview and cannot imagine a picture of the interviewer shaking your hand and congratulating you on getting the position, say words like successful, congratulations, new employee, etc. This can be a form of positive affirmation. It is little wonder that people who want to give up smoking are told to repeat constantly, *I am a non-smoker.* We are training the mind to have a certain image of ourselves that becomes part of our reality and experience.

We can use images or words to change our mood; for example, by recalling a pleasant experience, we can feel happy. Or, if we know we are stressed, anxious, or nervous about something, we can picture ourselves acting confidently, and as a result, will be more likely to cope with the situation.

Use the following short relaxation technique when you are stressed at work. Grab a cuppa, sit in your chair, close your eyes, and take yourself through this creative visualisation. A couple of minutes of this, and you will feel calmer and more able to cope with the rest of your day.

Exercise 10—Comfy Couch

1. Close your eyes and relax.
2. Recall the main living area in your home and the main pieces of furniture in the room.
3. Look at the shape of each piece of furniture and the colours.
4. Notice your favourite chair or lounge.
5. See yourself walking toward your favourite chair or lounge.
6. Now curl up into this comfy, warm, secure, familiar chair.
7. Stay like this for a few minutes, enjoying the imagery of being at home.

Visualising Your Future

Creative picturing can be used to help change your life for the better. If you are worried at work, unhappy in your relationship, wanting to pass the final year of high school or college, then you can utilise creative visualisation to help create a better future. What you see possible in the mind is possible to achieve because you must believe it before you will see it! Seeing yourself in a better place starts in your mind.

When my marriage of two decades ended, I was painting the internal of the house to spruce up before selling and moving on to a working holiday abroad the following year. I had music playing in the background, and I kept replaying a song by Savage Garden with the lyrics:

> *'I knew I loved you before I met you*
> *I think I dreamed you into life'*

What an affirmation if you are looking for a partner, 'I dreamed you into life'. What a powerful way of rewiring your brain with positive affirmations. After such a tragic end to a long-term marriage, I was so grateful that some years later a new partner did come into my life, and I often give thanks to this song for keeping my dream alive. Find songs that are affirmations of the way you want to live your life and sing them with all your heart. I find having them on my Spotify favourites and playing them in the car is the best way to keep reinforcing my goals and way of being.

Thinking, *I don't see myself getting a new partner* is not affirming. It is believed that one negative thought can take nine positive thoughts to counteract the mindset. To do anything, we must first see ourselves achieving it in our mind's eye over and over. Unless we have the inner chatter of, *I will get a great new partner*, we probably will not. It is not enough to think, *I can pass college*, because this gives you an option; you are capable but may not achieve this result. Can and will are two quite different instructions to our inner self. Developing a mantra, *I will graduate*, and saying it every time you sit down to study gives the right positive mental attitude towards studies. It is even more powerful when you add a time to the affirmation; for example, *I will graduate at the end of* ...

While rewatching a Star Wars film recently, I was impressed by Yoda and his teachings. I especially liked Yoda's response to Luke Skywalker saying he would give a task a try. Yoda responded, 'NO! Try not, DO! Or do not. There is no try.'[6]

Follow these four phases to help bring about change and achieve goals in your life:

Set the Goal

In the early stages of creative vision, avoid exceedingly difficult goals and choose a goal that you feel confident you can achieve if only you set your mind to it. Maybe the goal is to work hard at school or college this year and pass.

Picture the Goal

Now lie down and undertake the relaxation exercise learned during Session 1 audio. Once your body is relaxed, stay in this position and start to picture the goal. If you want to pass college, envisage yourself at the graduation ceremony. See yourself being photographed and freeze the frame and study your face at this point of achievement.

---

6 Star Wars: Episode V—The Empire Strikes Back. America 1980.

Think Positively

While lying down in the relaxation session, develop a positive phrase (affirmation) about your goal. Using positive affirmations, you can affirm yourself with positive self-chatter to help achieve your goal. For example, *I will graduate.*

Create an Action Plan

Now you need to plan steps that will ensure you achieve this future for yourself. So, in the example of graduating from high school or college, you can make a list of what it will take to get there.

Here is an example of making a commitment to the above-mentioned goal:

- handwrite notes
- have one daily file and transfer notes to subject file
- complete homework every night
- read a page, then review
- finish assignments before they are due
- summarise topics before exams.

Handwrite Notes

In class, take notes when listening to the teacher—this helps to keep focused, and handwriting helps the brain to remember.

One Daily File and Transfer Notes to Subject File

Use one daily file for all subjects with dividers to separate each subject. Ensure notes are placed in date order. This system helps keep everything easily at hand and lightweight. At the end of a topic in each subject, transfer handouts, class notes, exercises, etc. from the one file into a separate file for each course. Each course file could have dividers for each of the topics covered in the course.

Complete Homework Every Night

Set aside a time each day, for example, 4.30 pm–6 pm and 7 pm–8.30 pm. A break between two sessions is better than one long session where you will lose concentration. Decide how to utilise the time, e.g., first session for homework, second session for ongoing assignments.

Read One Page and Then Review

When reading texts, only read one page at a time. Go back over the page and highlight the most important points. Then jot the key points in the margin. This method will stop you from drifting off, and you are more likely to stay alert and digest what you are reading, picking up only the important points.

Finish Assignments Before They are Due

Always finish assignments a few days before they are due. This gives the subconscious mind time to go over your work. You might be surprised at the fine-tuning you are able to do when you proofread later by reading aloud.

Summarise Topics Before the Exam

Prior to exams, use a separate notebook for each subject and make summaries of each of the topics. Firstly, read and summarise your class notes. Secondly, read the textbook highlights and points in the margin, write a few sentences for each page and add these to your summary. Thirdly, summarise any handouts and exercises. Read your summaries in the notebooks often. Don't do this at the last minute but take the time necessary for good summary revision. This might mean giving up a weekend or two prior to the exams.

If you can make each course summary into a story that you can remember, it will improve your chances of recalling details in the exam. For example, if you are studying genetics in biology, make up a fictional story about a person that includes all aspects of the topic. Memorising this will be easier than trying to remember a whole lot of facts. Another way to take a topic into an exam, especially if it requires writing essays, is to write down the keywords and make them into a story. This way you will be able to recall the keywords and jot them down as soon as the exam starts, giving you the outline of your essay.

Getting Organised

Student Example

This well-organised system is a far cry from what one of my students had in Year 11. Towards the end of term one, I saw him enter the room with a piece of paper and a pen. He had no file, no textbook, no other notes. At the end of the lesson, I asked him where his notes were. He hunched his shoulders and had a lost look on his face. I walked with him to his locker as it was the mid-morning break. I gently asked how his other subjects were going and got the same nonchalant response. After further gentle probing, he owned up that he did not have a clue how to get on top of everything and felt totally overwhelmed by upper school.

I asked him if he would show me his locker, and I was taken aback when he opened it and out fell pages of notes, handouts, and books that were just all shoved into the locker. There was total disarray, books were clearly damaged, and there were no course files.

He didn't have a system, leaving him feeling overwhelmed and in a state of inertia.

I spent a few lunchtimes helping him get sorted, and he agreed to involve his mum to help him keep his subjects in order until he could get a handle on the system. Step by step, we found a way for him to feel in control of his studies.

He was the worst example of disorganisation I had ever seen, and I thought about the rest of my classes. From then on, the first lessons of my courses were spent sorting out a system with the students so they could be on top of the course.

The steps outlined above allowed all students to feel in control, no matter their level of previous organisation. This was the beginning of my students being organised in their workplace and homelife—it was a worthwhile life skill to teach.

I went on to write textbooks and completed a master's in educational management, where the dissertation was on formatting learning materials to assist student learning. I always had in mind how I could set out the book and what would help ensure all students, including the young man just mentioned, be supported through the courses.

Salesperson Example

As a TAFE lecturer in Managing Yourself in the Workplace, I would ask the adult students at the start of the course for examples of where they felt disorganised and what they wanted help with. A travelling salesman described the back seat of his vehicle as a tip, so I worked with him on how he could be better organised.

As a result, he bought a lever arch file, a concertina file, a three-drawer desktop box, a punch, three packets of alphabetical dividers, pens, white-out, and a diary. Whenever he left a client, he could punch any paperwork and put it under the correct alphabetical divider for that client. The A4 business diary had the week in view on the double-page spread, so when he visited clients, he would write anything he needed to know in the diary and mark future appointments. During workdays, he kept this diary on the passenger seat of his car. The concertina file was kept on the back seat, and in it he placed all the pamphlets, etc. that he needed for his business. The desk box kept things like pens, punch, and white-out, so they no longer rolled around the car and under the seats.

By the end of the term, he said he was amazed at how quickly he felt so much better about his work. He did not feel anywhere near as uptight now, and instead of just dumping everything on the back seat, it only took a minute to put everything where it needed to go after each visit to a prospective buyer. He saved time finding what he needed when on the phone or getting ready to go into the next business to sell his products. As a result, he said he felt more confident and now didn't feel embarrassed if his boss saw his car.

You don't need to be tech savvy to be organised; however, the salesman could buy a mini scanner for his car to scan all documents after each client. Or he could photograph the documents using his iPhone and AirDrop them to his computer, where he could have a file named Clients with sub-files for each client. Finally, he could keep his appointments on his computer and phone.

Getting organised takes a little time, but in the long run, saves a lot more time and helps you achieve mental wellbeing.

The Future is Boundless

In the early 1970s, the idea that everyone could one day have their own computer seemed far-fetched. Yet today, I am writing this book on a computer, saving the material in the cloud, and using a portal to submit documents. What an age we live in! These abilities were beyond the comprehension or imagination of mankind such a short time ago. Yet from our natural environment with its grass, trees, mountains, rivers, breezes, sunshine, waterways, and rocks, which are all simply different vibrational levels of energy and molecules, come these amazing devices. Who would have thought! Is it not wonderful that someone thinks of the unbelievable? Some people are not limited by the physical, by the improbable, but question *what if?*

Exercise 11—Believe It and You Will See It

1. If you can, have a friend help you with this exercise. They will need to have a pencil in hand.
2. Stand up straight with your back facing the wall. Your back needs to be about one and a half metres away from the wall. Place your feet about thirty centimetres apart.
3. Look straight ahead, stand very still, and raise your right hand and arm. Study your hand as you lift it up.
4. Once your arm and hand are outstretched in front of you, horizontal to the ground, hold that position. Focus on the index finger of the right hand as you point that finger. Maintain your attention on the index finger.
5. Very slowly indeed, move your right arm around to the back of your body, pointing your index finger. Keep moving the right arm as far as you can until your finger is pointing as far as it can behind you.
6. Now look across at the wall and make a mental note or have a friend mark where your finger is pointing.
7. Slowly return your arm to the front and let it drop to the side of your body.
8. Now repeat the exercise, but this time do not actually use your arm. Do the whole thing in your mind's eye. Visualise your index finger moving slowly around to the back of your body.

9. This time, when you reach the point on the back wall, visualise (in your mind's eye) taking the index finger much further around your body. See yourself stretching further around to a point along the wall.

10. Make a mental note of the position on the wall, which is much further along than the one you achieved in the last exercise.

11. Now slowly bring your imaginary finger back around to the front and pretend you are dropping your arm back into the same position in which you started.

12. Try the exercise again, but this time with your eyes open and carrying out the activity physically. Make a mental note, or have your friend mark the wall where you got to this time.

Do not read on until you have carried out this activity.

What did you notice? You will have been able to go much further in your final attempt because you triggered the mind with an image that it can do something better, and thus, the body carried out the instruction in action. Frequently, we limit our lives by our negative self-image or limitations of what we can achieve by our first effort. Using positive visualisations, we can achieve so much more!

No doubt you have heard the saying 'mind over matter'. The mind can control the body. We can trick the mind and make the body do things we once thought were beyond us. We can extend what we can do by mentally visualising the extension of the physical. I am not suggesting you visualise flying and then be disappointed when you cannot fly! I am suggesting that we can improve any performance in the physical by first seeing the achievement on a mental level. Hence the reason athletes picture themselves performing at top levels before they play the game. What you tell yourself and see yourself doing can become your future reality.

As another example, maybe you have told yourself you are an insomniac. Just by labelling yourself an insomniac creates a negative image of yourself as someone not able to sleep. A smoker trying to give up smoking does not use the affirmation, *I am a smoker*, instead, they use the label, *I am a non-smoker*, and thus they have a positive image to shape their view of themselves and what they can achieve, that is, giving up smoking.

So, if you are currently experiencing difficulties with sleep, do not label yourself an insomniac, instead, encourage the possibility of finding a way to sleep. By closing your eyes and imagining yourself at peace, rested, and able to sleep, you are triggering the brain to tell your body that it is agreeable for you to have a good night's sleep. Envisage getting out of bed in the morning feeling refreshed and ready for a new day.

The following practical session needs to be undertaken in bed and is designed to help you prepare for sleep. Your goal could be to have a restful night's sleep, so you need to create a snapshot in your mind's eye where you see yourself soundly asleep. Your affirmation could be: *I allow myself to sleep and awake refreshed.*

Consider the following ideas, which have been found to foster sleep:

- Have a warm drink (hot malted milk or chamomile tea) before bed.
- Avoid eating and engaging in screen time one hour before bed.
- Dim the lights in the house one hour before bedtime.
- Have a candle-lit warm bath with a few drops of lavender or bergamot oil.
- Go to bed at the same time each evening.
- Do not oversleep—this is part of setting your body clock.
- Have a comfy bed but do not overheat with too many covers.
- Open windows and curtains; fresh air and sensing dark and dawn aid sleep.

- If restless, get up and have a small snack (glass of milk, cheese and crackers) before returning to bed.
- Use Practical Session 5 as a guided relaxation for sleep.

Audio Practical Session 5: Sleep Readiness

You are now ready to listen to the practical session available on audio recording. Repeat this session many times over the week at a set time.

Session 6: Wellbeing

As you may have discovered during exercise eleven in Session 5, the mind is a powerful influence on the body. Is your body unhealthy? Have you resigned yourself to this state, or do you want to have a goal for a healthier body? Without a commitment of the mind, picturing the goal, affirming yourself along the way, and breaking down the steps necessary to undertake and achieve this goal, little may improve.

Mind Healing the Body

In the 1980s, a man came to our school to give a motivational talk to the upper school students. He had a serious bicycle accident and was told by his doctors that he would be paralysed and dependent on others for all his needs for the rest of his short life. He told us that he became aware of his situation in the hospital bed and felt that if he was to improve, he must not despair or resign to his lot. He made a pledge that he would never entertain a negative thought. He would affirm himself with positive thoughts. He worked tirelessly with his doctors, physiotherapists, and occupational therapists, pushing himself through everything they suggested. He set himself small goals and put all his energy into achieving those goals step by step.

Two years later, the man was moving his limbs, riding a specially designed low-to-the-road bicycle, and giving talks to the public in his broken but improving voice. He left our talk to continue preparing for a 1,000-kilometre charity ride across the Nullarbor Plain on a modified bike. His next goal was to walk within two years.

The cyclist went on to say that he not only used positive thoughts during his healing process but incorporated them into every part of his life. He felt it was important to have this holistic approach. If, for example, it was a cold and miserable Sunday, instead of complaining, he would say, something like, it's a perfect day for curling up indoors with a good book. He decided to only focus on positive thoughts, which bring up positive and healing emotions and wellbeing.

Does the above sound familiar? Remember the four phases suggested in the last session about the way to implement change? This man's approach is a testament to the power of positive thinking and highlights the healing ability of the mind.

This man could have been so miserable, but he wasn't. If we despair or bottle up our despondency, frustrations, and anger, it can lead to ill health. You may have heard of the very old saying, 'Vent your spleen'; in other words, release your anger before it does damage to your organs. Another saying is, 'They are a pain in the neck'; and here we are saying that someone's negative effect on us is causing physical pain to parts of our body. Does anyone give you a headache or low emotions when you are around them? Can you change the way you perceive others using mental images?

Exercise 12—Positive Emotions

If you are feeling down at times or need a lift, try the exercise below. It requires you to lie on the floor on your rolled out yoga mat and take yourself through a prone position relaxation. Use Session 1 guided audio if necessary.

Once you are relaxed, recall an incredibly happy day in your life. Maybe it was your birthday party, or a special dinner, your wedding, or a holiday. In your mind's eye, while lying down, replay the entire happy event. For example, think about your wedding day, recall getting dressed in the morning, the time with loved ones helping you, and the trip in the car. Recall walking down the aisle, hearing the vows you both took, the photographic session, replay the speeches, relive the reception, the dancing, cutting the cake, changing your clothes to leave for your honeymoon.

When revisiting a memory, like recalling an incredibly happy time, you will recreate the emotions attached to that day. This can be a vivid experience with pleasurable sensations, and the overall flow of energy is positive. The emotions created from remembering a pleasant event will wash over you and help change any negative feelings you have been harbouring, aiming to fill you with positive emotions to continue your day in an improved state.

As well as recalling a joyous event, you can be grateful for everything in your life. Even difficult people give you opportunities to learn and grow, so be grateful for this. Some families take time at the evening meal to say what they are grateful for in their lives. By introducing gratitude to your children, you are giving them a powerful emotional tool.

Gratitude increases your awareness of other things to be grateful for and can lead to higher levels of gratitude. Many benefits have been found from people who apply gratitude, such as decreased depression, higher levels of wellbeing, increased sleep quality, greater resilience, higher levels of academic interest, and lower levels of drug use.

Gratitude meditation focuses on acknowledging what you are grateful for in your life. It can help you cultivate a sense of inner peace and happiness.

Exercise 13—Gratitude Meditation

1. Try starting your day with some gratitude. Give thanks for the blessing in your life, i.e., being alive, having a job, a loving family, sufficient food to eat.
2. Do this while waiting for the jug to boil for your morning cuppa, or place a gemstone in your pocket and each time you feel it, give thanks for your life.
3. At the evening meal, take a moment to allow anyone at the table to give thanks and show gratitude for anything they experienced during the day.

Positive Speech

While criticising others, you avoid judging yourself. In the same way that people choose to focus on positive thoughts about their life, they can choose to avoid gossip and negative talk.

We all have faults, and drawing attention to another person's faults often occurs because we do not have a strong self-image. Highlighting others' faults takes the spotlight off your own but is not helpful in developing accountability in your own life. Maybe you would not cheat on your partner and feel you can judge another who has, but maybe you have cheated in another way. So as the Bible states, 'He that is without sin among you, let him first cast a stone at her.'[7] Judging other people implies that we are superior and without

---

7 New Testament: John 8:7.

fault when this is obviously not the case. If we are highly evolved and living a pure life, then we would have developed a great deal of compassion for those on the path and understand they are probably doing the best they can.

Walk a Mile in My Shoes

'Walk a mile in my shoes' is such a powerful statement about how we could be more compassionate instead of judgmental. If you grew up in a loving, supportive home where your parents ensured you were fed, clothed, and safe, then you are one of the lucky ones in this world. You may have been even more privileged if you received education at a tertiary level and lived in your parents' home until you could afford your own. If you have not been physically, emotionally, or sexually mistreated, you have had a fortunate life. Not all people are so fortunate; some are the product of an unstable, dysfunctional home base.

Compassion is the Key

The more love, acceptance, and compassion that goes towards even the worst delinquent, the more likely they are to internalise the positive image and aspire to this image. Show a person their true potential and they will rise to it. If you discard them as unworthy, they will act accordingly. We need to be generous in focusing on the positive things we see in others, and they will eventually flower.

We are all on a path. Some may be so far back on the winding road of life that we cannot see their path or notice any progress they are making. We can shine a light ahead for them and hope they will follow a more positive path in life. However, we must keep in mind that we are also travelling the path and still making mistakes along the way.

Positive Mind Leads to Positive Speech

To lead a positive, productive life, one first needs to live positively in one's mind. The more you take a positive view of the world and the people in it and have hope for humankind and our Earth, the more likely this is to manifest into reality. Inside all of us, we have the potential to change our future for the better. Positive comments to others and showing you believe in them can improve their belief in themselves as you are projecting an image of them to which they can aspire. When someone is lost, but you tell them the potential you see in them, you give them hope, and from hope comes action to improve themselves.

Control Over Emotions

We have control over our emotional state. How we perceive something is how it is.

For example, I saw a friend off at the airport as they were going overseas. Another of his friends who came to say goodbye was crying as she farewelled our friend, while I was full of smiles and joy. One person is happy, one person is sad in the same situation. The sad friend could have been thinking how much they would miss our friend, while I felt joy and happiness for his good fortune to travel and experience new things. Each of us can experience opposite emotional responses to the same set of circumstances because it is our mind that perceives things as happy or sad. We choose our response to a situation, no one can make us happy or sad.

Victim or Survivor Mentality

I once read about a group of people who were kidnapped and held captive for several months. Every night, the guards would ask them, 'Is there anything you would like?' Knowing the guards were unlikely to fulfil even their basic requests for nutrition, let alone any other request, they jokingly replied, 'A taxi out of here'. They would take joy in each day they were still alive. This helped them to evoke a scene that wasn't so dire, to allow them to survive until they were finally rescued.

We can get locked in, feel sorry for ourselves as victims, and not look for a way out—'Woe is me! Why is this terrible thing happening to me? I feel so angry, it's not fair!' Instead of focusing on being a victim, it can help us to focus on being a survivor.

Lemons or Lemonade

If life has dealt you lemons, try and make lemonade! I do not want to be trite about the terrible situations a person can find themselves in. I have experienced sexual assaults as a child and adult. I have feared for my life when threatened by a man with a rifle and an axe, who implied he knew how to get rid of a body so no one would find it. I have also experienced other aspects of domestic violence, such as gaslighting and coercion. I know it is not easy to make lemonade!

When my mother died suddenly, I had just started a relationship with a new boyfriend. I felt comforted by him, and he quickly suggested I move in with him. In this vulnerable state, I was silly enough to agree, and I paid the price for the next two years until the police helped me escape this toxic relationship.

I was so grateful to my sisters for taking me in and letting me just chill out. I barely left the house as I was so afraid my aggressor would be outside, and when someone knocked at the door, I would freak! I was suffering from post-traumatic stress disorder (PTSD). Having someone there with me was so helpful as I talked, slept, and reset to do the same the next day; it was like Groundhog Day for many months. I slowly followed my psychologist's advice to do anything other than lie there all day. She told me it was important to start going for a walk or to the coffee shop, even though it took a mammoth effort. Exercise is such an important part of recovery due to the chemical released to the brain during activity.

I had to keep reminding myself that everything is impermanent, even sad feelings. I held on to what my mother told me, that 'Life can turn on a sixpence'. I would just be with my feelings, let them rise and fall, not attach myself to them, and remind myself of the Buddhist understanding of impermanence. For example, the plant grows, it flowers, the flower dies, but its seeds allow another plant to grow. Nature shows us that life is all about change. We are never in a static state of being. The blossom will come again, spring is perennial.

For a few months, I moved interstate to stay with a very dear friend. He was marvellous; he would knock on my bedroom door every morning and insist I get up, and he would drop me at a gym en route to his work. Thank goodness he wouldn't take no for an answer and ignored my excuses! I did my workout at the gym and walked back to his apartment via a coffee shop. A feeling of being responsible for myself started to return, and I started to feel part of the world again. To my amazement, the psychologist was right, the low feelings were slightly better after doing something.

Taking medication was another way out of the darkness. There is such a stigma about being on medication for depression or anxiety. Everybody is happy for a person with a weak heart or with diabetes to take medication, but judge us if we take medication for the brain. I even had a family member say to me, 'Oh, you are taking your happy pills', and a friend said, 'Just buck up, pull yourself together'. I found it best to avoid such people and was grateful to those who were there for me. I had a rocky road on medication at first, as there are several different groups that treat the same condition. I'm so glad I persisted and eventually found the one that was just right.

During this time, I meditated daily and practised mindful exercises during daily chores. This helped keep the anxiety at bay and gave me a welcome relief from my situation. I eventually felt ready to undertake rapid eye movement therapy with the psychologist, specifically dealing with post-traumatic stress and was thrilled with the outcome. I no longer jumped when a stranger approached me or screamed if someone entered a room without me seeing.

These traumatic life events have taught me a lot and have helped me be more compassionate and understanding of others in grim predicaments. As a result, you can help others and appreciate more of the good things that happen later once you learn to start a new life.

Whenever I am feeling down, I try and give thanks that I am still alive and can look forward to another day, and who knows, it might be a better day. Sadness usually passes if you just let it be. I have never complained about getting old, but give thanks for every birthday and that I survived these traumas.

Life Could Always Be Worse

I once met a man who had lost both of his children. No parent should have to outlive their children. His daughter had been abducted and murdered. Then a couple of years later, his son was slipped the date-rape drug, had an adverse reaction, and died.

Some people have so much sadness in their lives and can be defined by that, but this father continued to get out of bed each day and lived as best he could. I felt so sorry for him and what life had dished up. We need to help one another any way we can, as many of us experience disaster at some time in our life.

Maybe you are not in such a terrible situation, or maybe you are living your own nightmare. Would you like to improve your lot? Plan a way out of whatever predicament you are in using the four phases taught in Session 3.

Anger

Most people get angry at some time. Anger is not a problem, it is what we do with anger that is important. If we take our anger out on another person in either a physical or verbal manner, then we are being irresponsible and not mindful. Going for a run, punching a boxing bag, or pounding into a pillow can release the tension. You might want to sit with the anger in meditation and allow it to rise and eventually fall, remembering that all states are impermanent and anger will pass.

Anger can be the catalyst for positive change. We can get so frustrated and angry about something that it propels us into action to change our circumstances. After we have been on our run or meditated, we can sit quietly and find a solution to what is causing the anger. You usually want to avoid feeling the anger again, so you look for a way forward. This might involve seeking out a good friend to discuss your problem, or it might mean seeking a counsellor to work on some solutions or changing something in your life that you have been procrastinating over.

Anger can often come from things not being the way we think they should be. For example, if you say to your partner, 'You should help me more with the children', realise you are trying to force your values on another. You cannot control another person or make them behave in a certain way. Often, we use the word should when we are angry because we have an expectation that everyone should share our perceptions and values. By changing your tone and asking, 'Could you help me more with the children', you are taking the sting out when talking to your partner. You are acknowledging that you do not look at the world the same way. Your partner might think that because he works longer hours, does the shopping and cooking, he is already pulling his weight and feels ill-equipped to manage the needs of the children. He thinks you should be doing it as you are better at ensuring the children are cooperative.

Walk a mile in your partner's shoes. Do not judge their actions but ask questions about where they are coming from and why they choose not to do certain tasks in the house. Discuss, don't argue! Look for middle ground. Find a way for each person to feel worthwhile. Accept your shortcomings and try to improve. Be more compassionate to others. Do not try to hide your faults from yourself by keeping occupied finding faults in others.

With practise, wisdom will arise. You will not feel so angry and may be more inclined to listen to others and different viewpoints. When you stop trying to prove yourself and feed your ego, you will not find it necessary to have the last word!

Exercise 14—Let It Be

An interesting exercise when angry is to meditate using the 'Let it be' meditation, which is the title of a song from The Beatles. Some words are as follows:

> *Let it be, let it be, let it be, let it be, let it be, let it be,*
> *Speaking words of wisdom, let it be.*

Make a commitment that when you are next angry or frustrated or have any negative emotion you would like to release, immediately go somewhere to meditate. Sit in the basic sitting posture and notice what the body is going through when it is expressing this emotion. Notice your facial expression, the frown, the tightness of the facial muscles, the pinched lips, the tension in the body, the knot in your stomach, the raised temperature, the rush of adrenaline. Notice and pay close attention to your body in its negative state.

As you inhale, feel the air cleansing you as it enters the body. As you exhale, imagine the body letting go of all this negative energy and allowing it to wash away. So, instead of focusing on the breath or counting numbers, we are focused on the emotion. Just feeling it.

During this meditation, it is important not to continue thought patterns that initiated the anger or frustration. If the emotion followed an argument with a loved one, do not continue thinking about them. It is crucial not to let the thoughts fester; the negative emotion will subside naturally as soon as you stop feeding the anger with negative thoughts.

After the angry feelings have subsided, notice the state of the body. It will be calm and peaceful if you have allowed the body to expel all the anger. When the anger has dissipated, it is time to start solving the problem. If you cannot think of a solution or are unsure, do nothing. Do not be reactive. Many people act for the sake of doing something instead of waiting for the solution to come to them through wisdom. When you have found a feasible solution, it will feel so right, and you will not have doubts, you will know it is time to act. You will feel mentally strong in your conviction.

Talking Not Listening

Too often, we think we are listening when we are just waiting to jump in and talk about our own experience. Frequently, we are too busy with our thoughts to be sure that we have understood the other person's point of view. Our mind is that monkey mind, all over the place and not focused on what we are truly hearing. We find out later, maybe when a partner becomes angry with us, that we have totally misunderstood what they were conveying.

This often occurs when a teenager is talking to their parent. Instead of listening carefully, mums and dads find themselves automatically value judging what their child is saying and only half listening because they think they have heard it all before. In this situation, one does not accept the other person for who they are and listen to what they are sharing.

Parents want to raise their children to be good citizens with high values. The best way to do this is for the parent to model that behaviour. We can set boundaries for our children to ensure their safety during their rearing. It is best to explain the reasons for these boundaries to your children. Talk to your children and explain what led you to adopt specific values and ideals. Children may ultimately end up (as adults) with different values to their parents, and we need to respect one another for those choices.

Mindful Listening

Another form of mindfulness is being totally present when someone is talking. Instead of concentrating on the breath, focus on what the other person is saying. Hang off every word the other person is saying, treating them as the most important person in the world in this present moment. If you are having a conversation with your employer, when they speak, be present and not distracted by other thoughts or judgements regarding what they are saying. If you are at home and your pre-schooler is telling you all about their day, be present, take in what they are saying, for you will never have this moment again.

Exercise 15—The Gift of Listening

Try this paired storytelling to raise awareness of your willingness to just listen.

1. Place two chairs opposite one another. Sit a volunteer opposite you. Make sure you can look one another in the eye. Be mindful of the other person's personal space (everyone has a different personal space).
2. Allow one person to talk about an event from their past or a place they have visited.

3. The person listening is not allowed to talk or add to the other person's story. They can't interject or request clarification. They can't add their own similar experiences. The listener is there to truly hear the speaker's story.
4. During your listening, be aware of body language. It is helpful if you nod, smile, and show facial expressions that reflect what you are hearing. Up to sixty percent of our communication is done via body language and not through the spoken word.
5. At the end of the experience, either feed back to the storyteller what they said in their story, share what you gained from the experience, or check in with them to see how correctly you interpreted what they were saying.
6. Only when the storytelling and feedback are complete can the listener offer their own experiences, should they desire to do so.
7. Now the pair swap roles, with one person speaking and the other listening.

Have I Heard You?

Unfortunately, when one person starts talking about their problem, they do not always identify the real problem. I have seen examples where one person starts to talk about their problem, and through active listing, they identify that the real problem is something quite different.

Active listening is like the above exercise but has one extra part. Again, you sit down and focus on the other person, carefully listen to what they have to say, use body language to show you are reacting to what is being said.

However, to truly actively listen, you also need to reflect to the speaker what they have said after a few sentences. Do not go off into a rage about what they are saying or accusing you of, but summarise back to them what you have heard (without value judgement or interpretation), and wait for their response. They might just nod in agreement and move on, or they might start to clarify. By adding this layer, instead of waiting to the end of the story, you are checking in every sentence or two to ensure you are both on the same page.

An example of active listening:

Woman: Why are you late home again?!
A wife tells her husband how annoyed she is that he is late home for dinner.

You might surmise that the woman wants the man home on time every night but let us see what happens when he does not react angrily or try to justify himself but actively listens. Let's start the interaction again.

Woman: Why are you late home again?!
Man: So, you hate it when I am late home at night?
Woman: Well, I do not mind it when you are late after playing golf with your brother.
Man: So, you do not mind me late from golf with Matt, but you do mind me going drinking with my colleagues?
Woman: Well, they are mainly single people and a lot of young women. I am not comfortable as I have seen Emily flirting with you in the past.

Now this opens a whole new problem. It is not him being late; it is her insecurity about Emily. He could have started an argument if he had snapped at the beginning and not actively listened to ensure he had the story right. With the right approach, people will often come clean about what their problem truly is.

Maybe in this situation, the woman was embarrassed that she felt so insecure and had trust issues with her husband. How often do we really say what we mean and mean what we say? The human person is a complex being. If we are more in touch with our thoughts and concerns, we may be more likely to be open, authentic, and honest with one another.

Regular meditation helps you to be more in touch with your inner self. Then deeper, more meaningful conversations can be had about issues in your life, instead of beating around the bush like the wife did in the above situation.

Exercise 16—Active Listening

Use the instructions in Exercise 15, but have each person talk about a problem they are willing to share.

1. Sit close at eye level and focus on the person talking. Use nods, smiles, facial gestures to show you are alert and attentive.
2. After the speaker has spoken a few sentences, the listener will feed back to the speaker what they have heard to check they are both on the same page.
3. Be prepared for the speaker to adjust what they said because when they hear it back, they often feel comfortable and listened to, willing to share the problem at a deeper level.
4. Remember, you do not have to be a problem solver. In fact, the more you try to solve another's problems, the more you disempower them.
5. Let them talk, listen, ask questions, and possibly at the end, if they are not closer to a solution, throw a couple of suggestions in the ring.
6. The more they are heard, the closer they will come to finding their own solution and feeling more capable.

The technique of active listening is especially helpful for solving problems. This does not mean that every communication in the household or workplace needs to take the form of active listening. If you want your pre-schooler to clean their teeth, you do not have to actively listen to their reason for not wanting to clean their teeth. Some instructions in the house are not up for negotiation. However, the more you meditate, the more present and mindful you are during your day, the more sensitive you become to the feelings of others and sense intuitively when there is the need to active listen.

Positivity

In the same way we can use communication techniques to improve our emotional and mental wellbeing, there are mental techniques we can use to improve and assist the body to heal. Just like the man who had the bicycle accident and pledged to only entertain positive thoughts of healing, you too can work with your mind to have a positive effect on your body.

In the practical session that follows, we will use a long relaxation session in the prone position. After relaxing all the muscles in the body, we will identify a particular part of the body to focus on. Maybe you get headaches, or digestive problems, or backaches or have a disease. During the practical audio session, you will hone the region of your body that needs attention. You are going to value add to all the medical advice and treatment you have been given by taking the mind to the area that needs your focus.

We are going to creatively visualise the area of the body that needs help and give it a shape and colour. For example, if you suffer from headaches, take your mind's eye to that region and sketch a black cloud in your mind. During the meditation, focus on the black cloud being that part of the head where you think your headaches occur.

Next, we will introduce a box. In your mind's eye, you will package the black cloud (that represents your headaches) and post the headache away. Say silently to yourself that you are sending this headache away. Now vision the positive energy you are creating in this area and allow your mind to wash the area in bright lights. You are affirming that you want to be rid of the headaches, and when you take the medication prescribed, you are also involving the mind and body healing.

You could also picture an infusion of golden beads entering your body with every breath that you take, entering the lungs and passing to the bloodstream. Imagine the beads being dispersed around the whole body. Clearly envisage the golden beads of goodness passing through all the veins and capillaries in your physical being. You could add the affirmation, *I give myself permission to heal my body.*

This does not mean you don't take medical advice or treatment; it means you are also going to focus your mind to direct the body to heal. One should never use mental exercise as a replacement for seeking medical advice or treatment, and I do not suggest that creative imaging is the answer to healing. It can be used in conjunction with other actions to improve your situation.

As well as medical assistance and meditation, one needs to be mindful of the way they are living their life. A positive mindset, balanced diet, and regular exercise are important factors for our emotional wellbeing and long-term health.

The Whole Self

If you want something to happen and improve, closely examine your life. Human life can be broken up into **intellectual, emotional, social, physical, and spiritual** growth. Intellectual growth is the desire to learn and develop our mental skills. Emotional and social growth is our need to be loved and accepted and to give love. We measure the emotional aspect in terms of our emotional IQ. We can be highly intelligent but emotionally immature. Physical growth is our ability to have a fit and healthy body and our willingness to exercise the body to function in a state of wellbeing. Finally, spiritual growth is finding truth, seeking our purpose in life, aiming to be in harmony with nature and understanding our place in the universe. If we have a deficit in one or more of these areas of our life, then our existence is disorderly and unbalanced.

Intellectual Growth

Do you use your intellect for the good of humanity and the earth? Using your intelligence to improve other people's lives and doing good for the planet is a meaningful way of living. We each need to be proud of what we do in life and how we are devoting our life's purpose.

Recently, I met a carpenter who had become disillusioned and left this work. He had built a wall in a house, and the inspector signed off on it and left. The builder then told him to take the wall down, as this would save money by not having to fit out the wall, doors, etc. The carpenter was worried because it was a load-bearing wall and he was concerned for the safety of the future occupants.

Imagine if all the carpenters walked off in this situation and felt strong enough to report the builder. As individuals, we need to act with integrity to improve our world. The more whistle-blowers there are, the more our world will change for the good and end the acceptance of corruption in our society. Bad things happen when good people do nothing!

Working in business management in schools and universities, I often helped young people with career choices. If they were confused, I would ask them to go back to their childhood and find out what they most enjoyed and how they passed their time. I sent some students off to talk to relatives about what they saw the child enchanted with in the early years.

If you were out in the garden with diggers, building roads, and moving trucks while your sibling was indoor colouring in and painting, you are probably gifted in quite different areas. Think about the different lessons at school and which ones inspired you. Examine your passion for living and what areas you think are most important. If you are working indoors but you yearn for the outdoors, or working with machinery but yearn to interact and help people, or in some way disappointed with your livelihood (like the carpenter), then examine your career path. Another way is to go online to the Australian Careers Service and take some tests such as JobQuiz.

It is important for your intellectual wellbeing to make opportunities that keep your mind active and alert. Consider joining a political party to utilise your intellect in making changes for our future. If you are disheartened by the state of our politics today, the only way to make change is to become involved. Join others trying to make our governments more responsible, accountable, and visionary.

Even if you are homebound, you can join courses online to keep your mind active. Books are a great way to expand your intellect, and joining a book club can take you to new places as you read material chosen by others. Mental exercises, such as crossword puzzles or sudoku, are a fun way to keep the cogs turning, and playing board games can help develop strategy skills.

Mental stimulation can be found in many ways, such as building models, playing chess, or joining a public speaking group or a peace movement. Studying literature, learning a new language, or commencing any course can open your mind to new possibilities and developments. Remember, team sports also make new connections in your brain, improving the capacity of the mind and increasing problem-solving skills.

Emotional and Social Growth

Humans need social interactions to develop their social and emotional intelligence. Having friends and family is essential to our social wellbeing. People to care for, and people to care about us, is part of a healthy existence.

Family and Friendship Circle

For most of us, family is where we feel safe and can express ourselves with confidence in a familiar setting with those we know and trust. Family helps us to develop the ability to interact effectively with the outside world. It is where we first learn the importance of love and caring for others and being part of a team. If you are without family, for example, working overseas, then it may be a time to develop stronger friendship bonds.

Our early adult life is often a time for developing friendships that will be part of our whole life experience. Around this time, we seek people who share the same morals, values, and standards as us, so we can feel comfortable and connected in their presence.

It's not the number of friends one has that is the measure of who we are, but the depth of our friendships. A couple of true friends who you meet with regularly can help develop your social intelligence—far more than many followers on social media!

One of the best ways to create a state of emotional balance is to not fret about having friends or a partner, instead, get out and do the things that show you love yourself, develop your self-esteem, and give you opportunities to connect.

It is not healthy to obsess over getting a friend or a partner, being liked at work, or being the centre of your family. An obsessive attitude and behaviour pushes others away, resulting in the opposite of attracting people to you. Once you focus on being calm, positive, self-reliant, and content, you will no longer emit that negative energy, and with a positive, harmonious energy, you may be surprised how quickly friends, colleagues, family members, and possibly a partner gravitate towards you. Radiating loving-kindness from within brings bees to the honeypot compared to grasping, needing, or desperate behaviour that drives them away.

During a hobby, you can genuinely be attracted to someone, and they can have the experience of getting to know you first as a friend and maybe feel that something extra is growing. This allows things to blossom more normally and allows the chemistry (scent, etc.) of one to alert to an interest in the other. None of this occurs on dating sites!

Leisure pursuits can be one of the most meaningful ways to find true friends. Join a political party, where you will meet like-minded people who share your aspirations for the community. Volunteer your time somewhere and you will meet people who care about others. Join a hiking/bike riding group to meet others interested in being fit and healthy. These are examples of natural ways of making friends and developing deep connections and far better than joining a 'singles group outing club' where the agenda is already set.

Seeking a Relationship

At one stage in my life, I had moved to a new town and was working way too hard. I was too lazy to make the time to join hobbies or become involved in the community. So as a quick fix, I went on dates from a dating app. After over 100 dates, I can assure you it is not a successful way to find a mate. There was just a lot of scrolling, emails, coffees, some lunches, and lots of disappointment! Meeting over the internet is mindless. I cannot remember how many coffees I paid for, or how many conversations about their last relationships I heard. I can't recall the number of scary moments as they insisted on walking me back to my car, or the number of lunches I purchased because I realised how hard up they were. None of it was good. And the worst thing was I got myself into an abusive relationship on about the 110th date!

I could have been more successful doing my hobbies and community work. In fact, when I did this and set about getting myself right, within a couple of months, I met my beautiful partner at the ocean pool. We were both doing our exercises and struck up a conversation about the condition of the water. I am still with him some fifteen years later and incredibly happy.

Volunteering to do something in the community that uses your passion and skills is an opportunity to meet people and possibly make new friends while helping others, the environment, or the planet. This is not about scrolling pictures on dating sites where the focus is on one thing. On a dating site, you cannot be sure of the other person's background or if they are who they say they are. Meeting people willing to give up their free time to do something for another is a sure sign the person has some honourable values, so that is a good start.

Taking up hobbies and giving back to the community helps you develop as a more balanced, content person who will not need to rush into anything. You will learn to enjoy your own company and what you have to offer and be more fulfilled when you have time at home alone. There will not be an urgency for rushing into friendships or relationships.

Life is full of twists and turns. You may not meet anyone through hobbies and volunteer work. Instead, you might make a close friend or two, and who knows, their single brother or sister might be introduced to you. Meeting a potential's family and friends is essential to ensure you find out the true person they are. On a date from an app, they can pretend to be all you want them to be, but meet their friends and family, and you will have an insight into the type of person they are. Do you like their friends? Are they good people? Meeting their social circle will help you understand far more than a dating app, where they can list what they like and create a whole other persona.

Avoiding Abusers

If your emotional intelligence is not well developed, then it will probably show up in your relationships and maybe also your work life. Learning to build yourself up to be aware of emotionally toxic people and how to deal with sociopaths in the workplace is just as important to your work life as it is to your personal life.

Prince Charming is to be avoided at any cost. If he charms his way into your life, he is probably too good to be true. He may have an abusive nature, where he charms you first and controls you later. He may wait until you are married, so date for many months and do not be in a rush to bed this person, as this can stop the continual evaluation you need to do to ensure the suitability of the partner. If they are not willing to wait, they are not the partner for you and do not respect you enough. Set your own standards, and you will attract someone with your values or at least someone who respects yours.

Abusers do not tend to keep up the charming facade longer than twelve months, so do not marry or become engaged or live with them during this time. It will help sort the good from the deceptive partner. Let them prove their worth; watch how comfortable they are letting you have your own space and friends, make your own decision, run your own finances, etc. Take your time to watch how they behave with animals, children, the elderly and how they treat their family members or an ex-partner. Do not kid yourself about them and only see what you want to see, be sure to listen to your intuition that will warn you. On your early dates, you could explain that you feel you have rushed into things before, and they have not worked out well, and this time you are determined to wait for several months before getting intimate. If they suddenly stop dating you, then you know they were not serious or respectful enough, and it is better to have moved on. Abusers are often sociopaths, and they are hard to spot initially. Even though they have no empathy, they can mimic it without sincerity when needed. This is how they trick people into trusting them.

Building Your Emotional Intelligence

To build your emotional intelligence, you need to build several areas. Work on your social skills by learning to be a team player and help others to rise. Actively put yourself in places where you must verbally communicate with others as this will help you communicate more effectively. Develop your empathy by becoming aware of those around you and identifying where they are coming from and understanding their viewpoints. This can be enhanced by using active listening to truly listen to others without judgement. Stand up for others who need your support.

Work on wanting success and accepting deferred gratification as part of building emotional intelligence. Control your impulses and avoid a quick fix. Work hard and find ways to improve your work and personal habits continuously, accepting that success takes time and effort. Have integrity in all that you do and be responsible for your actions. Be true to yourself. Stand up for yourself. Follow through on your promises and be honourable. Be strong enough to say no, as you cannot be everything to everybody.

Let other people be who they need to be, and do not allow yourself to be jealous of them. You are all separate trees in the same forest; other people are not a branch of your tree. Remember to let other people in your life fly, and if they come back to you, they do so with autonomy.

Importantly, accept that the world is changing, nothing stays the same, and be willing to accept change as a process of life. A willow bends to the winds of change and survives, but a rigid oak may snap in a storm. Be flexible. You cannot control life, only the way it affects you. Developing your emotional intelligence could determine your life's journey far more than developing your intellect.

Physical Growth

Food

Caring for yourself includes eating properly. You would not ignore the needs of your prized Ferrari and wait for it to break down. Your body is your Ferrari—it is the super quality vessel in which your spirit lives. Surely it would be a good idea to ensure it is getting the best fuel for the work it has to do? Are you eating a lot of pre-packaged or takeaway food? Are you cooking up quick meals full of fats and sugars? The Mediterranean diet (a way of eating that involves a great deal of fresh produce, small amounts of meat and olive oil) has been found to be the best for the health of your body.

Shopping, unpacking, preparing, and cooking takes up a lot of time, so if you want more time to meditate and care for your own needs, consider partaking in one of the many healthy meal kits that can be delivered to your door. These come with all the ingredients, the recipe, and they are quick and easy to cook. These kits take the stress out of evenings as the meals arrives once a week for the whole week. The ingredients come from local producers, are fresh and seasonal. When you think of the amount of food Australians waste, this is an economical alternative. Even the greenhouse effect from the delivery trucks is often offset by forest replanting by the delivery companies.

The portions are so generous that there is often enough left over for lunch the next day.

We even include a small fruit box for the week in the delivery. In our house, we keep it simple by only making porridge (great for the heart) for breakfast with yoghurt and fresh fruit on top. There is not much else to buy, and it has saved us money on food shopping with nothing thrown away or going limp in the fridge.

Aerobic Exercise

Do you exercise regularly? Are you involved in aerobic activity, such as swimming, skipping, running, fast walking, or bike riding for twenty minutes at least three times per week? This does not include the ten minutes of warm up and cool down that our bodies need. To ensure good health and fitness, make thirty minutes, three times per week about you. The first three weeks are the worst as we make every excuse possible to miss a session, but remember that after three weeks of sticking to a new routine, it becomes part of your life and not something you fit in. Remind yourself that if you break the routine during the three weeks, you will need to start your three weeks over again to ensure your brain is wired for regular exercise. Don't make excuses, just exercise!

Stretching

Do you do any stretching? Yoga is an excellent way to keep the mind, body, and spirit healthy. 'Yoga is a light, which once lit, will never dim. The better your practice, the brighter the flame.'[8] Yoga sessions are easily found on YouTube, so they don't have to be an additional expense. Or, if you want something more active, you could try tai chi, a derivative of kung fu that has the movements of martial arts but at a slow pace, where the focus is on perfecting each pose. There are eighty-five movements that can take years to learn fully, thus this is a journey.

---

8 https://www.catherineannisyoga.co.uk/yoga-quotes-bks-iyengar/

Spiritual Growth

Your spiritual life is the opposite of your material life. Your spirit is the opposite of matter and is affected by that which is not material or physical. This may mean your religion is your spirituality, but you do not need a religion to be spiritual. Some people think spirituality is about being in touch with God, the divine, the sacred. Others, who may not believe in God, embrace spirituality as being in touch with love, goodness, and all that is pure—that which radiates the brilliant light force of the Universe.

Spiritual means relating to one's thoughts, beliefs, and values. It is metaphysical, other-worldly, ethereal. Spirituality, then, is being in touch with our higher self, released from material bounds and seeking communion with the Almighty or the Universe or a life force. We will investigate this much further in the next session.

Audio Practical Session 6: Healing Focus

You are now ready to listen to the practical session available on the audio recording. Repeat this session many times over the week at a set time.

Session 7: The Soul and Spirit

O ur soul has its own personality and character traits. Hence, we sometimes say, 'He's a good soul.' It is self-centred and relates to our attributes, such as being kind, loving, and caring. When we act true to our inner core, we are more in harmony; we have a lightness of being and are more in touch with nature, caring for our planet, being kind, compassionate, and caring to all mankind. This can lead to feelings of peacefulness, authenticity, and tranquillity with wisdom emanating from us.

Should you seek to develop a good character and soul, Buddhism is one path that can be used, especially if you would rather follow a philosophy than a religion. Having said that, it still seems possible to me to be Buddhist and believe in God and consider yourself a Christian. As the Bible says, 'In my Father's house, there are many dwelling places'.[9] This has been interpreted to mean there are many different paths that lead to salvation.

---

9 New Testament: John 14:1-6

When seeking our higher self within and looking for the core of who we are, we might ask ourselves the following questions:

- Why am I here?
- What could I do with my life?
- How do I fit into the scheme of things?
- How can I bring harmony into my life?

During the practical session, I hope you will be more in touch with who you are, your purpose, your individual soul, and soaring spirit. Meditation will help you find peace, clarity, and insight.

Peace

Peace is quieting the mind to a point where you feel totally at ease. World peace starts with every family! If we do not have peace within ourselves, within our families, within our community, within our workplace, within our country, what hope is there for world peace?

A meditation that can be done to create peace is 'loving kindness' meditation. Here the focus, or mantra, is on saying silently, over and over, the words *loving kindness*. It is a little like chanting. One can also use creative positive thinking to imagine the love within us and allow this to beam outwards to the room, the street, the community and the Universe, generating loving kindness to all sentinel beings. To help start this loving kindness meditation, it may be helpful to remember giving a big hug to a pet you once had. Alternatively, visualise holding a baby, child, or adult who is dear to you and allow the love you feel for them to project from your heart into the world.

You could consider putting up a sign up in your workplace 'be kind'. Or start to sign letters or emails using the closure 'With kindness'. Maybe wear a necklace with the peace symbol to remind people of the need to strive for peace. We can all do our bit for world peace!

Clarity and Insight

Clarity is about seeing things as they really are.

A monk told the following interesting story.

> *A senior monk asked one of his disciples to concentrate on a bird on a perch some distance away and maintain focus on the beak. After a short time, he asked the disciple whether he was doing this, and the disciple answered that he was. Then the monk asked the disciple if could he see the right eye of the bird, and the disciple answered that he could. The senior monk sent the disciple away, telling him he had much to learn.*
>
> *The senior monk then trained another young disciple through the same exercise, and when he asked if the disciple could see the bird's eye, the novice answered that he could not. The senior monk asked him to explain, and the disciple answered that he could not see the eye because he was focused only on the beak, so he could only see the beak. The senior monk was thrilled and told the young disciple that he had learned a great deal.*

This is single focus where clarity is gained by not being distracted by other things and thoughts but being totally focused on the meditation object. To be useful, the focus must be on one thing at a time. For example, the question, 'What should I make my life's purpose?' Train the mind to focus on this question, and you will gain enormous clarity of thought. Disciplining the mind to be pinpointed will allow for much deeper thoughts and analysis than a mind wandering all over the place.

When we have controlled the mind and trained it to stay present and not wander, we are able to watch the mind from our higher selves and use the mind as a tool. Insight is knowing the moment the mind has drifted, then bringing it back to the present moment. We become the observer of our thoughts instead of at the whim and mercy of erratic thinking.

The monk told another story of a mother and child.

> *A mother was looking after her child, who was playing in the front garden near a busy road. The mother told the child to stay in the garden because of the dangerous road. The mother saw the child heading for the gate to the roadway. She could go up and punish the child or lock the gate. Instead, she patiently retrieved the child, repeating the instruction and watching the child. After gently but firmly bringing the child back into the garden many, many times, she eventually felt confident that the child would stay in the front garden.*

Once we have trained ourselves to stay with breath (the child to stay in the garden), it will eventually stay on the breath and not wander. Do not give up. Gently but firmly bring the mind back, as the mother brought the child back.

Living Mindfully

Our search for truth starts when we get to the point where we are the observer of our thoughts. Great insight comes and wisdom develops. Some people study religion for the meaning of life. All religious practices have meditative aspects, for example, prayer and saying the rosary. All religious practices have a code of ethics to live by. For example, Moses was given the Ten Commandments, which would bring the person to be more pure, authentic, and closer to Godliness. The Ten Commandments is one path you could follow:

Thou shalt:

1. have no other God except me
2. not worship false idols
3. not take the Lord's name in vain
4. keep hold the Sabbath day for rest and prayer
5. honour thy father and mother
6. not kill
7. not commit adultery
8. not steal
9. not bear false witness against another
10. not covet thy neighbour's belongings.

As a Christian, there is a belief that what you do in this life determines whether you go to Heaven or Hell in the afterlife. A life full of virtue following these commandments, would mean you could enter the Kingdom of Heaven.

For those following Buddhism, there are similar codes of behaviour to live by. For example, in Theravada Buddhism, there are five precepts that allow you to live mindfully and in harmony with all around you. The five precepts are:

Refrain from:

1. taking life
2. taking that which is not given
3. misuse of the senses
4. telling lies
5. self-intoxication of drinks and drugs.

Buddhists are encouraged to follow an eightfold path to enlightenment. The elements of the Eightfold path are qualities to be developed in the mind of a person who is seeking to secure an end to suffering and achieve the highest state of wisdom and happiness—enlightenment. The path relies on acting positively and purposefully for the right ends. Thus, one needs to develop the right:

1. View—understanding the nature of things found in the four noble truths
2. Intention—avoiding thoughts related to attachment, hatred, and harmful intent
3. Speech—not lying, using harsh or divisive speech
4. Action—refraining from physical actions such as killing, stealing, or sexual misconduct
5. Livelihood—avoiding work that directly or indirectly harms others, e.g. slavery, weapons, animal slaughter, intoxicants, or poison
6. Effort—avoiding negative states of being and sustaining positive states of mind that have arisen
7. Mindfulness—awareness of your body, feelings, and emotions
8. Concentration—single-mindedness.

The Eightfold path is shown as the Wheel of Life. There are eight spokes in the wheel, each representing one of the above right ways of living. Buddhism also reveals how important it is to lead a life on the middle path. For example, it is better to have a balanced diet than dieting one week because you have indulged mindlessly the week before.

When on a long retreat with the monks, I was woken at 4 am (the monks' time of rising every day!) by the beautiful, resonating sound of a gong. I would see others arrive at the ablution block looking as weary as me, and then we would make our way, in the darkness, along a little path to the meditation hall. We each took our place on the floor in the hall and sat crossed legged with eyes closed. Within a few minutes, a little bell would ring, and the meditation started. There was no meditation music to help relax the body or guided muscle relaxation exercises. Instead, you just sat with your legs crossed. I watched as thoughts came in, *I want to go back to bed; This is ridiculous getting up at this hour; What the hell was I thinking when I signed up for this.* However, as time passed, I noticed the thoughts were coming in less often. I eventually went to that place where you fall back from your thoughts, and I felt at one with the Universe.

Time passed, but I had no sense of it. After I don't know how long, the tinkle of the little bell brought me back, and the monk gently spoke and asked us to draw our attention back to the room. He asked if anyone wanted to finish now that we had meditated for an hour, and if so, they could get up and leave quietly. I was shocked we had been meditating so long. He continued to explain that if we would like to go for a further hour, then to stay seated. As I brought my attention back to the room and to my body, I realised I had a dead leg and could not move. Try as I may to move my leg, it just wouldn't.

Before I knew it, the monk was telling us we were now on our second half of the meditation, and I'd lost my opportunity to leave. I became quite stressed at the prospect of staying there any longer but had no choice, so I settled back into the meditation. I eventually lost connection with my painful dead leg, then my body, and went into the place where it is timeless again. Luckily when the monk brought us back from the end of the second hour, I noticed the discomfort of the dead leg had gone, but I was still so grateful to get up, move around, and go to breakfast.

Karma

Karma is important in Eastern philosophies where it is regarded as an energy. Just like we accept the law of gravity, many Eastern philosophies accept the law of karma. It involves energy from the first thought, which then leads into action, be it good or bad; this action comes back to the person in time, possibly through another person.

Karma is considered the divine system of justice, automatically creating the appropriate future experience in response to a current action. It is about cause and consequence and its relationship.

As it states in the bible, '... for whatsoever a man soweth, that shall he also reap'[10]. Karma also means that if you sow poorly, so shall you reap a poor crop. If you do bad things in life, this will more likely result in a bad outcome for you. There are usually consequences for one's actions!

Karma is the teacher that through the consequence, we are awakened to our poor choice of actions, and this can help us improve our behaviour or suffer if we refuse to take heed. Harsh karma can be a great spark for spiritual growth, an opportunity for one to turn their life around. Karma teaches us it is better to live a virtuous life.

Hindus believe there are three types of karma:

1. The sum of our past lives' karmas that need to be resolved.
2. The part of the karma that is experienced in this life.
3. The karma we are currently creating will possibly bear fruit in future lives.

Duality

In some ancient philosophies, duality is important. You may be familiar with the ancient Taoist philosophy symbol of Yin and Yang. The image represents the opposites in the Universe—night and day; male and female; hard and soft. The emphasis is always on balance, where one avoids the extremes.

In Eastern religions and philosophies, there is a clear understanding of the duality that is all around us. There are always opposites, for example, light and dark; good and bad; strong and weak. Therefore, they argue that if there is mortality, there also must be immortality.

10 King James Version of the Bible, Galatians 6:7

This is part of the law of duality. We are born and then we die, but given there is an opposite to everything, then mortality must also give rise to immortality. Interesting thought!

Reincarnation, Heaven, and Hell

Immortality takes the form of reincarnation in Eastern philosophies. As mentioned above, our unresolved aspects of karma in previous lives and those aspects of karma in our current life lead to reincarnation in a future life. This is designed to help us learn to resonate at a higher level of consciousness. According to reincarnation theory, where we are on the current path is the result of where we have come from in an earlier part of this life and previous lives.

The idea of reincarnation is supported and can possibly help explain a child genius. For example, a child star on the violin could be that way because they have spent many lifetimes perfecting their ability on the violin.

Reincarnation may also help explain how two siblings can be so different in personalities. Often personalities seem apparent as young babies. It is almost as if they were born with a predisposition, or it could be explained as the sum result of past experiences of karma.

Also, the feeling of déjà vu could come from having lived several lives. Something feeling familiar because we have lived it before could be an explanation. Hence, the feeling that you have been to an event or place you have never been before is because you may be reliving the event or place.

Finally, we have all had situations where we are introduced to someone new, and we immediately feel extremely comfortable with them. We can quickly carry out meaningful conversations with them as if we have known them all our life. We feel an instant connection and a sense of trust with the person. This is merely our first impression, but it is interesting that we often find, years later, that our first impression was right. Could it be that energy or magnetism attracts us to people from previous lifetimes? If we do reincarnate, it seems beneficial to keep living lives with people we have always been around. We would learn the most from sharing our lives with familiars. Thus, it is unlikely we will come back as an ant!

Reincarnation is believed to continue until we reach a stage of enlightenment; that is, we no longer have a need to return to this plane of existence because there is nothing left to learn and no need to be reborn. We transcend earthly boundaries, and the person's soul is freed from the bondages of their physical body. This is when we enter a state of Nirvana, which also fits with the idea of Heaven in other religions. Until the enlightened person passes over, they are great teachers for those around them who seek the path to enlightenment.

In Islam and Christianity, there is no such belief in reincarnation. Instead, one goes to Heaven or Hell when they die. Good deeds predict one's heavenly experience, whereas bad deeds mean one is destined for Hell. Thus, reincarnation has similarities to Heaven and Hell in that life after death is predisposed by the life you live this time.

Enlightenment

To reach the stage of enlightenment is to have such wisdom as to be free **from attachment, desire, and aversion.** This person is no longer suffering, as it is believed our suffering comes from our attachments, desires, and aversions. It requires the person to recognise that all is impermanent; that as something arises, so shall it fall. The following are the three root causes or poisons preventing the arising of enlightenment within the soul. They are the three afflictions or character flaws in humans. To gain liberation, one needs to develop wisdom, generosity, and loving kindness; and leave attachments, desires, and aversions behind.

Attachment

Attachment is a falsehood; power is a falsehood—they are delusions. For example, whatever relationship we are attached to, the other person can detach themselves from us; it is an illusion to think we have power and control over another indefinitely. We cannot insist someone stays with us forever. They may choose to, but they may also choose to leave us. We need to have the grace and wisdom to not put ownership on our relationships. If a partner wants to leave the relationship, they should be allowed to do so. You certainly would not set your partner and children on fire as a Brisbane man did some years ago!

Domestic violence would not exist if people were enlightened, understanding they do not own anything or anyone and that displaying power and control over another human being is only going to drive them away. It is a delusion to think you have power over anyone or anything. You cannot make someone stay with you; you do not own any living soul. You are confused if you think you are in control of the world around you. The opposite to this delusion is **wisdom,** which needs to be developed to have a wholesome way of living and overcome attachment.

Desire

Desire is an endless dark path to travel. If you are caught up in desire, the chances are when your neighbour or friend purchases a better car than yours, you will want something better. Keeping up with the Joneses is not part of the path to enlightenment. Being grateful for everything you have, and not needing material possessions to make you happy, is the path to peace and contentment. Gaining joy from repurposing, recycling, and reusing are all ways of defeating envy and ceaseless desire.

A sensual attachment to pleasure is ultimately sure to fail. Chasing the next fashion or the latest technology or lusting after the next relationship is doomed to continual frustrations. This is all so transitory and a meaningless way to live. Desire can lead to addictions and, ultimately, it is full of suffering. It does not feed your spirit and soul.

The opposite to desire is **generosity,** which needs to be developed and is a wholesome way of living if you want to overcome endless desire, greed, and seeking sensual comforts. Finding ways of giving and being generous of yourself for the benefit of others is genuinely fulfilling and satisfying.

Aversion

You must overcome aversion on your path to enlightenment. This relates to hatred, hostility, or ill-will for another, which gives rise to aversion. This is the basis of wars. Aversion to others leads to anger and hostility towards them. Living at peace with all is the way to overcome and feel compassion and understanding for others. This is the path for acceptance of all other peoples. The opposite to hatred and ill-will is **loving kindness,** which is needed to be developed and is a wholesome way of living if you want to overcome hatred and ill-will.

To sum up, being free from suffering, having wisdom, generosity, and loving kindness allows one to live with inner peace, joy, and contentment. This is the path to enlightenment. Once a person reaches this enlightenment, there is no need to return to this physical, earthly realm. They become immortal, living in a state of Nirvana.

Exercise 17—Scented Candle and Flower

1. Set out a glowing frankincense candle (or a candle and burn frankincense stick or oil burner). Also set out a flower or two in a little vase.
2. Relax in the sitting position with your eyes closed during relaxation.
3. Slowly open your eyes and take your attention to the light of the candle. Focus on the light as it spreads out from the candle. Watch as it flickers.
4. Turn your attention to the smell in the air. The scent of frankincense permeating the room. How does it make you feel?
5. Take your attention to one of the flowers. Study the structure— the shape, the colours, the petals, the symmetry.
6. Allow wonder to arise in the amazement of nature. As you sit and focus on the flowers, say a prayer for nature, our planet, and all creatures living on Earth.
7. Chant, 'Wisdom, generosity, and loving kindness'. Send this prayer out to all and include yourself in receiving wisdom, generosity and loving kindness.
8. Finally, reflect on what you could do tomorrow to increase your wisdom, show your generosity or give someone loving kindness.

Preparation for Audio Practical Session 7

During the practical for Session 7 on audio, it is important that you find a place in which you feel at one with nature. When I am taking a group of students through this part of the course, we usually meet at the bottom of a hill in the afternoon and hike to the top to view the sunset over the land. You might prefer to watch the sunset over the ocean.

Take a torch, blanket or cushion, jumper, track pants, runners or walking shoes, and mobile phone (make sure you have access to the audio Session 7). Take a picnic hamper. It might be sunny and warm when you leave in the afternoon, but the temperature drops when you meditate, as well as when the sun goes down. Make sure you arrive at the place in time for sunset (once you start the meditation at sunset, the sun is usually gone within ten minutes).

In quiet contemplation, walk to the top of the hill or along the beach to your rock, observing all that you see along the way. Avoid trivial chatter. Do not treat your walk like a task. Do not try to get to the top first. Stop along the way to observe a bird or gaze at a crumpled leaf on the ground. Be interested in the process and walk in a meaningful way in the present.

The idea of spiritual meditation or part of a spiritual retreat is not limited to a one-off situation but can be something the whole family or a group of friends can engage in. It is uplifting to spend some of your holidays camping or in close contact with nature. To sit silently with your family to view a sunrise or sunset is a special, shared experience. These are moments long remembered, as are hugging a tree, floating in a river, or being the only one on the beach.

After the meditation on the sunset or sunrise, the whole family or group of friends could partake in the picnic and discuss their experiences, bringing the group together before walking back to the place where you all started. Without the distraction of screens and work, you can reflect, talk about goals ahead, and focus on a better way of being. During these spiritual meditations or entire spiritual retreats, you can ask yourself, *What is my life's purpose? What do I want to do with the rest of my life?* This is a wonderful family ritual to do on the last day of every year.

Audio Practical Session 7: Spiritual Connection

You are now ready to listen to the practical session available on the audio recording. Repeat this session over the week.

Session 8: Summary— Gateway

This book aims to improve your life, to bring balance, and teach you how to live more mindfully. The practical, mindful exercises and meditation practices stepped you along a pathway showing how to take a confused, busy mind, and develop it into a calm, concentrated mind full of clarity.

The sessions started by outlining the origins of mindfulness and meditation, including identifying some of the challenges and revealing how these can be overcome. Each session included an explanation of a particular area of life to be sorted and set out practical exercises to be completed. Guided practical audio sessions enabled the different practices to be incorporated and experienced in daily life.

Although three traditional methods of meditation are covered in this book—the prone position, sitting, and focused walking—there are many opportunities during chores and other daily routines to discipline you to act more mindfully. This included teeth cleaning, having your first cuppa, breakfast, etc.

It was shown that it is possible to complete sixty minutes of mindfulness and meditation per day, with little change to your existing schedule. This routine can go on a stick-it-note on your bathroom mirror as a way of making a commitment to include mindfulness and meditation each day. These practices can become as regular as getting dressed in the morning, as they become part of your normal routine. The first three weeks are the hardest, so keep at it. Once you have completed twenty-one days of consistently including these practices, they become entrenched. Giving in means you need to start the three weeks again, so don't give in! A daily routine for developing mindfulness could be observed during the following:

Exercise 18—Daily Mindful Practice

- Eat your daily breakfast in noble silence
- Have a cuppa in a garden after work
- Be mindful when you are cleaning teeth
- Rise slightly earlier and meditate.

In the later sessions, we moved on to include other focus techniques for examining problems in your life: setting new life goals and how to achieve them; being a better communicator; and caring for your body by consciously choosing a healthy lifestyle.

Living mindfully allows individuals to take full responsibility for their actions and makes them accountable for what happens in their life. Eating well, exercising, carefully listening to others, setting goals and planning their implementation are all part of designing the life you want to live.

Training the monkey mind (the mind with constant erratic chatter) is indeed a useful pursuit, as it leads to thinking with clarity and wisdom. This means you are more present in every aspect of your life, whether it is listening to someone, making love to your partner, or noticing an opportunity to help someone else.

Developing the ability to meditate can lead to higher states of being, where eventually the meditator will be the observer of their thoughts. Individuals can work towards being able to watch their thoughts as they arise and fall. This allows the extinguishing of negative thoughts or patterns before they manifest. Insight and clarity develop, and you are no longer chasing those never-ending, unquenchable wants. Instead of constantly manoeuvring to better our toys, it is replaced by a generosity for others, which results in a more satisfying life for everyone you meet. This is the path to enlightenment.

Meditating as a student for some fifteen years before teaching mindfulness and meditation in my mid-thirties was very helpful to my life. The more I use meditation, and the more I teach others, I refine the art and deepen the experience. I have had many fine teachers and learned a great deal. I passionately enjoy passing on this knowledge. I still regard myself as a student of meditation.

Being in a room of people meditating is a powerful experience, with a sense of bond and peacefulness. I encourage you to repeat what you have learned in this book and audio session joining a weekly meditation class. If you want to undertake the course again, but over Zoom, enrol in the course where you will interact with the teacher and other like-minded people. Please go to my website <www.zoomintomindfuness.com.au>.

I also encourage you to attend meditation retreats. My favourite is a Theravada Buddhist style retreat, but there are many others. I suggest that you complete this course before embarking on a retreat, as sometimes the length of time of the meditation sessions is not necessarily for the novice (especially five-day retreats). When you are ready, start with a two-day retreat. Over the years, I have found these retreats have often been a catalyst to the next level of benefits and experiences from meditating. They are wonderful opportunities to evaluate your life and decide on the next pathway.

There are eighteen exercises in the book, and they are well worth revisiting as a way of regularly examining your pathway in life.

Although in the early period of meditation you need to take the time to relax your body before focusing on the breath, as time passes, you will find sitting in the yoga position or lying in the prone position will trigger your body to relax, and you will quickly slip into a meditative state. If you have ADHD, it may take longer to gain the results but keep at it.

By using mindfulness during your chores daily, including it in communications, and using it to problem solve, you will start to see that over time; you are more focused throughout your day. The more you train the mind to be centred, the more you will do things to the best of your capabilities.

Continue to practise, and you will achieve wisdom, generosity, and loving kindness. You can experience a blissful state of being. You will be the observer of your thoughts, living in a higher, more meaningful state of being.

Being present in the present—what a present that is to yourself!

Introduction to Audio Practical Session 8

Now that you have used all the practical audio sessions, you might like to take your body through its own relaxation, then experience one of the following sessions throughout the week. You could mix it around, completing each of these over four consecutive days and then repeat. Or you could choose the one you think most benefits you on the day. This audio covers the following earlier sessions:

Audio Practical Session 8: Four Meditation Practices

You are now ready to listen to the practical session available on audio recording.

Session 1   Prone Position—focus on breathing
Session 2   Sitting Position—Zen counting
Session 3   Walking—focus on sensations of movement
Session 6   Body Nurturing—focus on healing

Appendix A

SESSION	BOOK Explanations, Instructions, & Exercises	AUDIO Practical Session
1	Introduction to Mindfulness and Meditation Exercise 1 Peaceful Mind Exercise 2 Moments of Peace	**Prone** position relaxation and focus on the breath
2	Overcoming Difficulties Exercise 3 Managing My Life	**Sitting** position and Zen counting
3	Active Meditation Exercise 4 Simple Task	**Walking** with focus
4	Reducing Stress Exercise 5 Cuppa Break Exercise 6 Teeth Cleaning Exercise 7 Eating Mindfully Exercise 8 Hobby Exercise 9 Music Relaxation	**Garden** messages
5	Creative Visualisation Exercise 10 Comfy Couch Exercise 11 What is Possible	**Sleep** readiness
6	Wellbeing Exercise 12 Positive Emotions Exercise 13 Gratitude Meditation Exercise 14 Let It Be Exercise 15 Listening Not Talking Exercise 16 Active Listening	**Healing** focus—body nurturing
7	The Soul and Spirit Exercise 17 Scented Candle & Flower	**Spiritual** connection
8	Summary—Gateway Exercise 18 Sixty Minutes Daily Practise	**Revisiting prone,** sitting, walking, and healing

Appendix B

Recommended Reading List

- *It's OK That You're NOT OK* by Megan Devine
- *Minimalism: Live a Meaningful Life* by Joshua Fields Millburn and Ryan Nicodemus
- *Tantric Sex: Step-by-Step Guide to Learning the Art of Tantric Sex* by Jim Owens and Grace Mason
- *The Ultimate Sex Book* by Anne Hooper
- *Emotional Intelligence* by Daniel Goleman PhD
- *Daily Wisdom for Why Does He Do That: Encouragement for Women Involved With Angry and Controlling Men* by Lundy Bancroft
- *Beating the Workplace Bully: A Tactical Guide to Taking Charge* by Lynn Curry
- *The Art of Disappearing: The Buddha's Path to Lasting Joy* by Ajahn Brahm
- Emotional intelligence short course <https://cce.sydney.edu.au>

Lightning Source UK Ltd.
Milton Keynes UK
UKHW020638231122
412703UK00017B/720